SENTIMENTAL JOURNEY

HOME TO HEATHER CREEK

SENTIMENTAL JOURNEY

Kristen Eckhardt

Home to Heather Creek is a trademark of Guideposts.

Copyright © 2024 by Guideposts. All rights reserved.

This book, or parts thereof, may not be reproduced, stored in a retrieval system, or transmitted in any form or by any means, electronic, mechanical, photocopying, recording, or otherwise, without the written permission of the publisher.

The characters and events in this book are fictional, and any resemblance to actual persons or occurrences is coincidental.

Scripture quotations in this volume are taken from the King James Version of the Bible and Holy Bible, New International Version®, NIV® Copyright © 1973, 1978, 1984, 2011 by Biblica, Inc.® Used by permission. All rights reserved worldwide.

Published by Guideposts
100 Reserve Road, Suite E200
Danbury, CT 06810
Guideposts.org

Cover by Lookout Design, Inc.
Additional design work by Müllerhaus
Interior design by Cindy LaBreacht
Typeset by Aptara, Inc.

ISBN 978-1-961125-19-3 (hardcover)
ISBN 978-1-961125-21-6 (epub)

Printed in the United States of America
10 9 8 7 6 5 4 3 2 1

This book is dedicated to the men and women
who served in World War II and the families
who loved and supported them.
Peace be with you all.

Home to Heather Creek

Before the Dawn

Sweet September

Circle of Grace

Homespun Harvest

A Patchwork Christmas

An Abundance of Blessings

Every Sunrise

The Promise of Spring

April's Hope

Seeds of Faith

On the Right Path

Sunflower Serenade

Second Chances

Prayers and Promises

Giving Thanks

Holiday Homecoming

Family Matters

All Things Hidden

To Love and Cherish

A Time to Grow

Sentimental Journey

SENTIMENTAL JOURNEY

Chapter One

Charlotte knelt down by the mailbox post and carefully shifted the loose soil around the delicate clematis she'd just planted. A couple of dark purple flowers already bloomed on the spindly vine. She'd carefully woven the plant around the wooden post, eager to see it in full bloom. Clematis was one of her favorite perennials, and she knew it would soon vine its way up and over the mailbox, creating a pretty display all summer long.

The sound of car tires on gravel made her look up to see the mail carrier headed toward her on the road. Todd Svoboda drove a green Subaru that got him around the rural route no matter what the weather.

She rose to her feet as the Subaru slowed to a stop in front of the mailbox.

"Hello there, Charlotte," Todd greeted her, his elbow resting out the open window. "I see you're spending this fine Tuesday morning doing some gardening. You're not planting a honeysuckle vine, are you?"

"No," she said, moving closer to the car. "It's a clematis."

"Good thing. I'm allergic to honeysuckle. I break out in a rash every time I touch it."

"That sounds awful."

"Itchy too." He handed her a thick bundle of envelopes sandwiched between some mail-order catalogs. "Looks like you're pretty popular today."

She laughed. "Looks like mostly bills to me."

"Well, bills are like rain," Todd told her. "They fall on the just and the unjust."

"So true. You have a good day, Todd."

"Same to you, Charlotte." He edged the car away from the mailbox, stopped again and leaned out the window. "Hey, tell Bob thanks for stepping up to the plate last night. We couldn't do it without him."

Todd sped away before she could ask what he meant. Bob had attended a meeting of the Bedford Volunteer Fire Department last night but hadn't said much about it when he'd come home.

As she walked back toward the house, Charlotte wondered exactly what her husband had stepped up for and how much work it would be for her.

She began thumbing through the mail after she walked through the door, intrigued by the large, thick envelope at the back of the pile. She flipped past the bills and looked at the label. It was addressed to Sam from Grand Island Print Shop.

"Finally," she said aloud, setting the mail on the table. They'd been waiting weeks for Sam's graduation announcements to arrive. He was graduating in less than three weeks, barely leaving her enough time to address all the invitations and send them out.

She hesitated, wondering if Sam would mind if she opened them. It wasn't personal mail, and she did need to get the ball rolling. Besides, she couldn't wait until he got home from school to see them.

Charlotte slipped into a chair and then edged her index finger under the loose corner of the envelope flap. She slit the edge and tipped the envelope far enough for the cellophane-wrapped package of invitations to slide out onto the table.

"Oh," she breathed, tearing away the cellophane. They were folded, cream-colored card stock with embossed silver and royal blue lettering. The front of the invitation carried a picture of a cougar, the school mascot, in the center.

Charlotte stared at the announcement, trying to make herself believe this was really happening. Sam was graduating and would be going out into the world on his own. The school year had flown by, and she'd assumed she'd be ready to send him off when the time came. But she wasn't ready. In her opinion, Sam wasn't ready either. He still wasn't sure what he wanted to do with his life—unlike Bob or Pete, who had both known they wanted to be farmers since they were boys.

But ready or not, Sam was graduating. She had the proof right here in her hands. Taking a deep breath, she opened the card to read the words inside.

The Senior Class
of
Bedford High School
announces its
Commencement Exercises
Saturday afternoon, May twenty-second,
two o'clock
Bedford High School
Auditorium

Class Motto
There is a difference between knowing the path
and walking the path:

Class Flower
White Rose with Blue Tip

Class Colors
Royal Blue and Black

She read it twice, her gaze lingering on the class motto. "There is a difference between knowing the path," she said slowly, "and walking the path."

She knew the right path by reading the Bible, but walking it wasn't always easy. Sam's graduation might be bittersweet for her, but she knew God would watch over him.

Train up a child in the way he should go, Charlotte thought to herself, remembering the words of Proverbs 22:6, *and when he is old he will not depart from it*. The verse gave her comfort, and she prayed that she and Bob had given Sam all the love and nurturing he needed to find his way in life.

Charlotte set the card back on the pile with a small sigh, wondering where she'd put the invitation list that she and Sam had compiled a few weeks ago.

A loud thump sounded above her, and Charlotte looked up at the ceiling.

"What in the world?" she muttered.

It almost sounded as if something had landed on the roof, and her mind flashed back to last week when she'd stepped outside and seen a large raccoon scratching at the steel roof of the grain bin. Her loud shout for Bob had chased the raccoon away, but she'd been surprised a raccoon could climb that high.

Surely a raccoon wouldn't be on her roof . . . would it?

Another noise sounded above her, confirming that it wasn't her imagination. Charlotte pushed her chair back from the table and stood up, trying to figure out what was going on. The kids were all in school, and Bob was helping Pete plant soybeans on the North Quarter.

That left her alone to discover the source. She marched up the stairs, stood on the landing, and noticed the ladder to the attic had been pulled down. Now she was really worried. Could someone be up there? She was sure the attic's trapdoor had been closed the last time she was upstairs.

As she stood listening, another strange creak sounded above her, followed by two more loud thumps. There was no doubt about it now. Something or someone was definitely in the attic.

She grabbed a broom out of the closet in the spare room and then headed up the ladder, not sure what she would find up there. When she poked her head through the trap door she heard a strange shuffling sound inside the room. She pulled herself up through the opening so she could see the entire room.

"Bob!" she exclaimed in surprise, seeing her husband bent over a box.

He jumped at the sound of her voice, almost tripping over an old phonograph behind him. Bob reached for the wall to regain his balance.

"What are you doing, sneaking up on me like that?" he grumbled.

She leaned the broom against the wall. "I thought you were a raccoon or an intruder."

He blinked at her. "Why in the world would you think I was a raccoon?"

She shrugged off the question. "I heard a strange noise up here and thought I should investigate."

His eyes moved to the broom. "And you brought that for protection?"

"I was going to use it to nudge whatever critter I found up here back outside," she replied, laughing now at the thought. "I certainly wasn't expecting to find you. Aren't you supposed to be in the field with Pete? I didn't see you come back in."

"That's because I drove up through the pasture to check the fan on the grain bin that was giving us trouble earlier. Then I decided to pick up a snack before I headed back to the field."

"You won't find any snacks up here."

"I got sidetracked." Bob turned back to the box in front of him. "I'm looking for Dad's World War II uniform. I know it's got to be up here somewhere."

The dust in the air tickled her nostrils, and she sneezed. Charlotte wondered why Bob needed his dad's military uniform, but she knew asking him more questions would only keep the two of them up here longer.

"It should be over here," she said, heading toward the opposite end of the attic. "That's where we put all your folks' stuff after your mom died."

Bob followed her, his work boots landing heavily on the hardwood floor of the attic. That explained the loud thumping sounds she'd heard from below.

The two of them began rearranging boxes until they found the ones that had been neatly labeled by Ma Mildred when she was still alive.

"Here it is," Charlotte said, reading the label on the top of the box. "Lester Stevenson, World War II."

Bob took the box from her and opened it. There were several old copies of the *Bedford Leader* on the top. He moved them aside and dug deeper.

"I got it," he said, pulling the faded khaki uniform out of the box. He lifted the wrinkled shirt up with one hand and the pants with the other. "This will be perfect."

"Perfect for what?" Charlotte asked him.

"The fire department is sponsoring a World War II reenactment for Memorial Day. I told them I'd help organize it."

Charlotte placed her hands on her hips. "So that's what Todd meant when he said you'd stepped up to the plate last night. I wondered what he was talking about."

Bob shrugged. "Somebody had to get this thing off the ground." He held the shirt up in front of him. "Think it will fit?"

Bob was built like his father but had grown a lot stouter over the years.

"I don't know," Charlotte said, trying to be diplomatic. "Your dad was a young man when he wore that. It looks like it might be too small for you."

"Well, let's find out."

She watched her husband take off his work shirt and then slip his arms into the sleeves of the khaki uniform.

"Looks like it fits to me," Bob said, as he began to button the shirt. But as his hands moved lower, the shirt began to gape across his belly. He couldn't button the last three buttons.

"It must have shrunk with age," Bob muttered, looking down at the shirt in dismay.

Charlotte didn't think that was the problem, but she decided not to say it aloud. "The length on those sleeves looks perfect."

"Yep," Bob agreed, looking down at the cuffs. He picked up the pants again and held them up to his waist. "The length on these looks just right too."

Charlotte was touched by the fact that Bob wanted to wear his father's old uniform in the war reenactment. "I could make you a uniform just like it. We could even use the same buttons and . . ."

"No need," he interjected, taking off the shirt before carefully placing the uniform back into the box. "There's no reason I can't lose a few pounds before Memorial Day. Dr. Carr has been nagging me to lose some weight anyway."

Charlotte doubted Bob could lose enough weight in the next few weeks to fit into the uniform, but she wasn't about to discourage him from trying.

"Why don't we take the box downstairs," she suggested. "I can iron the uniform, and the kids might like looking at the old newspaper articles and such."

"Good idea." Bob leaned down to pick up the box. "There are some old letters and postcards Dad sent home from overseas in there too. Maybe there will be some information in them to help us stage the reenactment."

As Charlotte followed her husband downstairs her mind was already coming up with low-calorie dishes she could make for supper. The kids might balk at them, but she'd make sure they had something they liked too.

It wouldn't hurt her to lose a few pounds either, she thought to herself. In fact, it would probably help both of them if they teamed up to lose weight.

The more Charlotte thought about it, the more excited she was about helping Bob fight the battle of the bulge.

Chapter Two

Sam leaned against his locker, waiting for the Tuesday morning bell to ring. Only nineteen more days left until graduation, counting today. Fourteen days if you didn't count the weekends. He couldn't believe he was almost free of this place. Sometimes it seemed like he'd be stuck here forever.

"Hey, Slater," Jake said, walking up beside him. "Only nineteen more days."

"I know."

"We are going to have so much fun on the senior trip. I can hardly wait."

Sam couldn't wait either. Every year, the seniors planned an overnight trip and left on their last day of school. This year they were going to Lincoln to stay at the Cornhusker Hotel. They'd be able to do fun things like play laser tag, paintball, and miniature golf. It was especially cool because the other classes were still in school for about another week after that.

"I heard there's a new skateboard park in Lincoln," Paul said as he approached them, his blue backpack slung over his shoulder. "I think we should definitely check it out while we're there."

"We'll have to get an okay from our chaperones," Jake replied, "but I bet they'll let us go. I think that park is close to our hotel."

"I wish today was the last day of school," Sam said wistfully. "I'm going nuts sitting in class."

"I know," Jake concurred. "It's not like they're going to fail us now; we've probably learned everything we need to know."

"It's all about control," Paul said. "Like when I got two weeks of detention for riding my skateboard in the hall. I can't believe Ms. Simons would rat me out. She's such a—"

"Hey," Sam interjected before Paul could continue. "She's my aunt now, and her name is Mrs. Stevenson. She was just doing her job."

"It happened after school," Paul grumbled, obviously still upset about it, "and if you ask me, teachers should be off duty by then."

"In a few weeks we'll never have to worry about detention again," Sam said. "In fact, we'll never have to step foot in this place again."

"That sounds great to me," Paul said, "but what are we going to do to leave our mark?"

"What do you mean?" Sam asked.

Paul stepped closer to the other two boys. "I mean, we need to come up with a great senior prank, something that will become a legend at Bedford High. We may want to forget about this place, but I don't want anyone here to forget about *us*."

Jake grinned. "Count me in."

"What kind of prank do you have in mind?" Sam asked.

Paul shrugged. "I don't know. I haven't thought of one yet."

"We could grease a pig and let it run loose in the school,"

Jake suggested. "Wouldn't you just love to see Principal Duncan try to catch it?"

"The greased-pig prank has been done a million times," Paul said with a wave of dismissal.

"Yeah," Sam agreed. "I think my grandma's senior class even pulled that one."

"So you come up with something," Jake challenged Sam. "Something nobody's ever seen before."

"Yeah," Paul said. "Maybe something from California. What kind of pranks did they pull back there?"

Sam hesitated, trying to remember his school days in San Diego. They seemed so far off it was almost like a dream. "I don't know."

"C'mon, think, Slater," Jake implored. "We need something totally awesome."

Sam was drawing a blank. "Give me some time. I'll come up with something."

"I know," Jake said, his eyes lighting with mischief. "We could glue all the lockers shut. No books and no pencils equal no school."

"And if they find out it's us, we'll have to pay to get them unglued—or worse, have to do it ourselves." Paul shook his head. "No thanks. I've already spent too many hours cleaning the skid marks from my skateboard off the floor."

"Maybe we could do something at the prom," Sam suggested. "We could wear crazy clothes or dye our hair orange or something."

"That won't work," Paul said. "My mom wants to take pictures of me and my date before I leave for the prom, and she won't let me out of the house if my hair is orange. Besides, Laurine would kill me."

Laurine Kelly and Paul had been dating only a couple of weeks. Sam suspected Laurine wanted a date for the prom more than she wanted a boyfriend, but Paul didn't seem to care about her motives. His mom had threatened to set him up with a date if he didn't find one himself.

Now that Sam and Arielle were back on solid ground he was looking forward to a drama-free prom night. It had to be better than last year, when he'd gotten sick and passed out at the dance after taking too much cold medicine.

"C'mon, guys, the bell's about to ring," Jake said, glancing at the clock. "What are we going to do for our prank?"

"We could put worms in the lockers," Paul suggested. "That would freak out the girls, for sure."

Sam nodded. "That'd be pretty funny."

"No, no, no!" Jake cried. "We've got to think of something big. Bigger than worms and bigger than glue and bigger than orange hair."

The boys all thought for a moment, oblivious to the other students milling around them. Sam wondered if he should ask Uncle Pete for ideas since he was always talking about what a troublemaker he'd been in school.

"I've got it," Jake said, snapping his fingers. "You know that old clunker Buick that's parked in a pasture near the highway just south of town?"

"Yeah," Sam replied. "I pass it every time I drive to school and back. What about it?"

"Well," Jake continued, "we could find a way to hitch it onto my pickup and haul it into town. Then we could put it right in the middle of the football field. We could even put a dummy dressed like Principal Duncan in the driver's seat."

Sam laughed. "That's pretty good."

Paul's eyes widened. "Hold on. I've got an even better idea."

"What?" Sam and Jake asked in unison.

The first-period bell rang, forestalling Paul's answer. He turned to Sam. "Do you think you can get a key to the school from Ms. Simons . . . I mean, your aunt?"

"I don't know," Sam said, wondering what Paul had in mind. "You mean steal it from her?"

"I mean *borrow* it. Just don't let her know that you did." Paul took a step away from them. "We'll need a key to the school to pull this off."

"To pull what off?" Jake asked him.

Paul grinned, walking backward down the hallway. "The greatest prank in the history of Bedford High."

WHEN CHARLOTTE WALKED INTO Fabrics and Fun that afternoon she was greeted by the fragrant aroma of cinnamon; she spotted a small loaf of cinnamon bread on the counter.

"Come on in," Rosemary called out to her. "I'm just about to have a cup of tea. Would you like to join me?"

"I'd love to," Charlotte replied as the door closed behind her. "Have you been baking?"

Rosemary nodded. "I froze several loaves at home a couple of weeks ago and decided to heat one up today. That toaster oven I keep in the back room is so handy. Would you like a slice to go with your tea?"

"I'd love one," Charlotte said, eyeing the loaf on the counter, "but I really shouldn't. Bob and I are starting a new diet today."

"I'll make it a thin slice," Rosemary promised her, picking up the knife next to the plate. "You don't have to tell Bob. It will just be our secret."

Charlotte smiled. "All right, I can't resist. I'll take half a slice. Maybe I can walk it off tonight after supper."

She watched Rosemary slice the bread and place the portions on two small paper plates.

"You can set these on the table," Rosemary said, handing the plates to Charlotte, "while I get our tea."

Charlotte walked over to the corner of the store where Rosemary had recently set up a table and chairs for customers to look through pattern books or just sit and visit. Charlotte plucked a stray thread off the green-vinyl tabletop and then set down the plates.

Rosemary soon joined her at the table with two cups of tea. She set one in front of Charlotte before sitting down across from her. "What brings you into town today?"

Charlotte leaned closer to her. "I'm on a covert mission."

Rosemary's eyes widened. "That sounds intriguing. Will you let me in on the secret?"

"Bob's volunteered to help organize a World War II reenactment as part of the Memorial Day remembrance ceremonies."

"Oh, I know all about the reenactment," Rosemary replied. "It sounds like a big job to me. Does he realize how much work he's taking on?"

Charlotte smiled. "We both know Bob's not afraid of hard work. The problem is . . ." Now that she'd come to the reason for her visit it was difficult to find the right words.

"What?" Rosemary asked gently.

Charlotte took a sip of her tea before continuing. "Well,

Bob dug out your father's old World War II uniform, and he's determined to wear it for the reenactment."

Rosemary's brow crinkled. "Will it fit him? Dad was twenty years old when he wore that uniform and, judging from the pictures, pretty slender."

"The length on the sleeves and pants is just right, but the uniform is too small around the waist for Bob. He couldn't even get the shirt buttoned when he tried it on this morning."

Rosemary chuckled. "Did he lie down on the bed like I do to get my jeans to button?"

"No, he didn't go that far." Charlotte smiled as she picked up the slice of cinnamon bread and took a bite. "But he's determined to lose as much weight as he needs to fit into the uniform."

"But Memorial Day is only about four weeks away. How much weight does he intend to lose?"

"At least ten pounds, maybe more. The thing is that Bob's tried dieting before and hasn't always been successful. May is such a busy time of year for us on the farm; he's been helping Pete as much as he can. Just last week he hooked up the herbicide sprayer and drove the tractor down to Sawchuck's Quarter to get the field ready for soybeans."

Rosemary nodded. "It's always go, go, go at planting time, and that usually means grabbing whatever food is the most convenient."

"That's right. Even though Pete's doing most of the work on the farm now, Bob pitches in whenever he sees something that needs to be done. The next few weeks are going to fly by, so I'd like to have a backup plan just in case Bob doesn't lose enough weight to fit into the uniform."

Understanding dawned on Rosemary's face. "You want to make a uniform that fits him, just in case. Is that the covert part of your mission?"

Charlotte sighed. "Yes. I'm committed to helping Bob lose weight, but we've been down this road a few times before. I'd hate to see him not be able to take part in the reenactment because he doesn't have a uniform to wear."

"I think it's a wonderful idea," Rosemary told her. "Besides, if Bob *does* lose enough weight to fit into Dad's old uniform, you could always sell the one you make to someone else. I've already got three orders to make uniforms for the event myself."

Charlotte leaned forward. "Does that mean you have a pattern for a World War II–style uniform?"

Rosemary smiled. "I surely do. I ordered some as soon as I heard about the reenactment, and several people have already been in to buy them. I've run out of khaki material, but I've got more on order. It should be here any day."

"Good," Charlotte replied. "I'd like to get started on it as soon as possible. I've still got Sam's graduation invitations to send out and his party to plan."

"You must be so proud of that young man."

"I am," Charlotte agreed. "I have to admit, there have been a few times when I didn't think we'd make it this far, but the Lord helped us through."

"Amen."

Charlotte took a sip of her tea and leaned back in her chair. "So what's new with you?"

"Well," Rosemary said with a long sigh, "it seems volunteering runs in the Stevenson family. I got talked into serving on the events committee for Memorial Weekend. This town is going to commemorate our veterans in style."

"Good for you."

"Say, Charlotte," Rosemary said, a twinkle lighting her eye, "your mother was in the USO, wasn't she?"

"She certainly was. I loved hearing her stories about it when I was a little girl. She had the time of her life."

"Then I think you'd be the perfect person to chair the USO–style dance we're planning for Memorial Weekend."

"Oh, no!" Charlotte exclaimed, holding up both hands. "I've already got too much on my plate with Sam's graduation and sewing a spare uniform for Bob."

"You can recruit other women to help you plan the dance, and if you agree to be the chair, I'll sew Bob's uniform for you. That way it will be easier to keep it covert."

Rosemary had a point. It might be difficult to keep her sewing a secret from Bob, and she didn't really want to sneak around the house with it.

Rosemary seemed to sense that she was wavering. "Please say you'll do it. I know the dance will get done right if you're in charge. I have too many other things to work on and I'm not even sure I'll want to go to the dance."

Charlotte found it difficult to turn Rosemary down, especially when she knew it would be a chance to honor women like her mother who had contributed so much on the home front during the war.

"Okay," she said at last. "I'll do it."

Chapter Three

Charlotte was just setting the last plate on the table for supper on Tuesday evening when a surprise visitor walked through the door.

"Do you have room for one more?" Bill asked, greeting his mother with a bear hug.

"There's always room for you," she told him. "So what brings you here on this fine evening?"

"I had a meeting in Harding and it took longer than I expected." Bill slipped off his suit coat and draped it over his arm. "So I thought I'd drive through Bedford on my way home for one of your home-cooked meals."

"Well, I'm glad you did," Charlotte said. "How are Anna and the kids?"

"Fine. Will has been battling a cold, so Anna took him to the doctor. Turns out he has an ear infection."

"Oh, dear," Charlotte replied, sending up a silent prayer for her five-month-old grandson.

"The doctor prescribed an antibiotic, and Will seems to be feeling better already."

"Well, that's good to hear," Charlotte replied as the clatter of footsteps sounded on the stairs.

Bill grinned at the noise. "Sounds like a herd of elephants."

"Just two growing boys," Charlotte replied as Sam and Christopher entered the kitchen.

"Hey, Uncle Bill," Sam said and then turned to Charlotte. "Is it time to eat yet?"

"Almost." Charlotte slipped on an oven mitt to remove her casserole from the oven. "Why don't you call your sister and grandpa in for supper. They're both outside somewhere."

"I'll do it," Christopher volunteered, racing toward the door.

While Charlotte finished setting food on the table, Bill walked over to the hall closet and hung up his suit coat.

"You were prone to ear infections too," Charlotte told her son when he walked back into the kitchen, "especially whenever you had a cold."

Bill smiled as he sat down at the table. "I remember you used to put that awful-smelling stuff on my chest whenever I was sick. What was that?"

"A mustard poultice," Charlotte said, placing the salt and pepper shakers on the table. "Ma Mildred swore by them. I'm not sure how well it worked, but at least it made me feel as if I were doing something to help you feel better."

"How about you?" Bill said, turning to Sam. "Has senioritis hit you yet?"

Sam leaned back in his chair. "I think it hit me last September. It seems like I've been waiting forever to get out of school."

Bill grinned. "I remember the feeling. The closer it gets to graduation, the more the days seem to drag."

The back door opened, and Christopher walked inside, followed by Emily and Bob.

"I saw your car in the driveway," Bob told his older son. "Are you staying for supper?"

"I sure am," Bill replied as Charlotte filled Bob's coffee cup.

"Pete will be joining us too," Charlotte told him, "because Dana has a meeting at school tonight. But he said to start without him if he's still in the field."

When everyone was settled at the table, Bob bowed his head to say grace. "Heavenly Father, we thank Thee for this food and for the blessings of this day. May we use those blessings to do Thy will. Amen."

"Amen," Charlotte murmured and then lifted her head to see Sam wrinkling his nose at the main dish.

"What is that?" Sam asked.

"Mushroom-barley casserole," Charlotte said. "I got the recipe from Hannah. It's supposed to be healthy and delicious."

Bob looked around the table. "Where's the meat? I thought we were having fried chicken tonight."

"That was before you and I decided to go on a diet," she reminded him.

"Oh, that's right," he said sheepishly.

"This casserole is both low-calorie and low-fat," Charlotte told them. "Hannah said it's very filling too."

Emily looked at the side dishes of spinach salad and cooked carrots, her face lighting up with delight. "So you made a completely vegetarian meal?"

"That's right," Charlotte said. "We won't eat vegetarian every night, but eating lots of fruits and vegetables helps you feel full without adding pounds."

Sam looked over at her. "Just because you guys are dieting, we have to suffer too?"

Bill choked back a laugh as he reached over to scoop up

a generous serving of casserole. "I'm sure if you made it, Mom, it will be good."

"Don't worry," Charlotte told the younger boys. "I have lunch meat in the fridge. You can make yourselves sandwiches if you're still hungry after dinner."

"Ham?" Sam asked hopefully.

She smiled. "Ham and roast beef. I've got some of those nice, thick buns you like too."

"Cool," Sam said, reaching for the casserole. "Although I've been craving roast lamb lately." He grinned at his brother. "I guess we'll have to wait until after the county fair for that."

"We're not eating Magic," Christopher told him. "So forget it."

"Magic?" Bill echoed, looking around the table. "Is that your 4-H lamb?"

Christopher nodded as he speared a tiny mushroom with his fork. "Yeah, he's a Suffolk lamb. They're supposed to be one of the best breeds to show at the fair."

Bob turned to Bill. "Christopher's trying to lead Magic around on a halter, but the lamb seems to be the one leading Christopher around most of the time."

Bill chuckled. "So Magic is dragging you around the farm?"

"Sometimes," Christopher admitted. "He's pretty strong, but I'm working with him every day. My 4-H leader said the members who have their animals trained to lead on a halter can be in the 4-H petting zoo at the park on Memorial Day."

"Oh, how fun," Emily exclaimed. "We can dress Magic up in red, white, and blue. Maybe I could even sew a cute little outfit for him."

Christopher grimaced. "I don't want you to embarrass him. Or me."

"Oh, it will be fine," she said with a wave of her hand. "He'll look very patriotic."

"It won't matter how he looks if he's not halter-broken," Bob told them. "The last thing you want to be doing is chasing a lamb around town."

Charlotte noticed that her husband kept glancing at the refrigerator. She wondered if she'd made a mistake in mentioning the lunch meat in front of him, especially when she knew how much he loved sandwiches. She'd have to make sure he didn't sneak out of bed tonight for a midnight snack.

"I know," Christopher told his grandfather. "I'm going to Dylan's house tomorrow after school and get back that dog training book I loaned him. Maybe there's a training method in it that will help me figure out how to lead Magic."

"Or maybe we should get a mule," Bob said, reaching for his coffee. "I remember a guy who used a mule whenever he wanted to halter-break a calf or a lamb. He'd put the halter on the animal and then tie the other end to the mule." He took a sip from his cup. "No matter how hard the calf or lamb pulled, the mule wouldn't budge. But if the mule wanted to go somewhere, the calf or lamb had no choice but to follow along."

"That must be where they get the phrase 'stubborn as a mule,'" Charlotte said.

"That reminds me," Bill said. "What's keeping Pete?"

The kids laughed, and even Charlotte smiled a little. Pete's stubbornness was well known in the Stevenson family. Once he set his mind to something, there was no changing it.

"That's what I'm starting to wonder too," Charlotte replied, looking over at Bob. "Shouldn't he be in by now?"

"He still had quite a few acres left to plant on Sawchuck's Quarter when I drove by the field this afternoon," Bob said. "He'll probably be here shortly."

"Then I'd better help myself to more of this casserole before it's too late," Bill said, spooning another helping onto his plate. "It's not too bad, Mom."

"Thanks," she said, hoping that was a compliment. "I think it's rather tasty myself."

Both Sam and Christopher made a face, but Emily piped in, "Me too."

Bill looked over at Bob. "What's with the diet? Did Dr. Carr put you on it?"

"No," Bob replied. "I put myself on it. The Bedford Fire Department is staging a World War II reenactment, and if I want to wear my dad's old uniform I need to lose a few pounds."

"What's a war reenactment?" Christopher asked. "Do you get to use guns and grenades and stuff?"

Bob shrugged. "I don't know all the details yet. We've got a meeting tomorrow with a group from Grand Island that performs these reenactments all over the Midwest. They're going to give us a how-to lesson."

Charlotte hoped there weren't any guns involved, at least not any with live ammunition. She was certain Bob wouldn't allow anything dangerous, especially since he was in charge.

"I'd like you boys to join in," Bob said, spearing a baby carrot on his plate. "My dad served in that war, fighting the Germans, so I think it's only fitting that the Stevensons should be well represented."

"Count me in," Bill said. "Sounds like fun."

Bob looked over at Sam. "How about you?"

Sam shrugged. "Sure, I guess. As long as it's not too lame."

"What about me?" Christopher asked. "I count as a Stevenson man, right?"

Charlotte bit back a smile at the question; yet, given the way Christopher was sprouting up, it wouldn't be long until his voice deepened and he started shaving.

"I'm sure we can find something for you to do," Bob told him.

Christopher grinned, obviously happy to be included. Emily, on the other hand, didn't look very happy. She leaned back in her chair and folded her arms across her chest.

Charlotte was distracted from her granddaughter by the loud rumble of a tractor outside the house.

"That must be Pete," she said, rising from the table to set another plate. "The planting seems to be going fairly smoothly this year, so he should be able to participate in the reenactment too."

"The weather's been just about right," Bob agreed. "Once Pete is done planting, all we'll need is a rain or two to give the crop a good start."

Charlotte stood by the coffeepot, waiting for Pete to come inside so she could ask him if he wanted a cup. But instead of the familiar clomp of his work boots on the mud porch, she heard the roar of his pickup truck. She walked over to the window and looked out just in time to see him tear out of the driveway and head toward Bedford.

"Where's he going?" she asked.

"Maybe he figured there wouldn't be any food left when he saw my car in the driveway," Bill joked.

"Maybe," she murmured, letting the curtain drop from her hand. It wasn't like Pete to take off like that, especially when he'd told her to plan on him for supper.

"Or maybe Uncle Pete heard we were having mushroom-barley casserole for supper," Sam said, evoking laughter from the rest of the family.

Charlotte laughed too. "I suppose that's possible. Pete is more of a meat-and-potatoes man."

"So am I," Bob said, setting his napkin on the table. "But I guess I'll have to give up the good stuff until after the war reenactment."

Emily slumped in her chair. "I don't think it's fair that girls can't be included."

"Girls didn't fight in the battles," Sam reminded her. "Only men could be soldiers back then."

"But women still contributed a lot to the war effort," Charlotte told him. "They worked as nurses and ambulance drivers overseas and took the place of men in the factories here at home. Then there was the USO . . ."

"People all over also planted vegetable gardens," Bob said. "They called them victory gardens."

"What's a victory garden?" Emily asked.

"A big vegetable garden. Almost everybody planted one so there wouldn't be a shortage in the food supply. That way there was plenty of canned goods and such for the boys at war."

"They also served as morale boosters," Charlotte said. "Planting a victory garden made people feel like they were helping with the war effort without leaving their own backyard."

"So if I can't take part in the war reenactment, I can

plant my own victory garden instead," Emily mused, "just like the women used to do back in the old days."

Charlotte smiled. "I think that's a wonderful idea. In fact, I might suggest that to Rosemary. She's on the Memorial Day events committee, and that would make a great community project."

"Well, I'm going to make *my* victory garden an organic one," Emily announced. "No chemicals of any kind."

"Hope you like bugs," Bob told her. "They like vegetables even more than you do."

"Don't worry, Grandpa," Emily replied. "I'll find a way to keep them off my plants without using sprays or any of that other nasty stuff."

"Sounds like it's going to be pretty busy around here," Bill said pushing his plate away, "what with planting season, Magic, Emily's victory garden, Sam's graduation, and the war reenactment. It almost makes home seem peaceful, even with three little ones around."

Charlotte smiled. "You can add planning a USO dance to that list. Your Aunt Rosemary recruited me to chair the dance committee when I stopped by her shop today."

"What's a UFO dance?" Christopher raised an eyebrow.

Everyone laughed as Charlotte started explaining it to him. "No, it's a U-S-O dance. USO stands for United Service Organization. Its mission is to support the troops, and it's still in existence today. My mother volunteered for the USO when she was just a little older than Sam. She always said it was one of the best times of her life."

"How is a USO dance different than a regular dance?" Emily asked her.

Charlotte thought for a moment. "Well, the USO sponsored dances near military bases in the United States and invited soldiers to offer them a little recreation and entertainment. I suppose we'll all dress like they did in the 1940s and do the dances that were popular back then."

Bill rose to his feet. "Then I'd better get home and practice my jitterbug. Thanks for supper, Mom."

"You're welcome anytime." Charlotte walked him to the door. "Say hello to Anna and the kids for us. And take good care of that baby."

"I will," he promised, giving her a hug before heading outside.

Charlotte stood in the open doorway, watching Bill climb into his car and then pull out of the driveway. She could hear the rest of the family back at the table talking about the reenactment, but she wasn't ready to join them again just yet.

She was worried about Pete, remembering the way he'd shot out of the driveway. It reminded her of when he was a hotheaded teenager and peeled out like that whenever something made him mad.

She sighed, aware that worrying about your children never ended, even when they were all grown up. Pete had a wife to take care of him now, but that didn't mean Charlotte couldn't apply her favorite home remedy, one that came straight from the heart.

"Please watch over Pete, Lord," she prayed softly, "Protect him and bless him and give him peace. Amen."

Then she closed the door and walked back inside.

Chapter Four

Later that evening, Charlotte padded out of her bedroom, quietly closing the door behind her so she wouldn't wake Bob. Still worried about Pete, she'd been tossing and turning in bed for the last hour. He hadn't answered his cell phone and she didn't want to bother him at home. She'd confided her concern to Bob after the kids had gone to bed, but he'd brushed it off, certain that Pete was fine.

"Pete probably just forgot he was supposed to stay for supper," Bob had told her. "He's got a lot on his mind these days, what with building the house. He's got to keep on top of those carpenters. Plus, he's busy with planting, and those early calves need to be weaned soon."

She knew he was right. Bob had even been pitching in more than usual to help Pete with chores and repairs. No doubt Pete would stop in for coffee in the morning and they'd all have a good laugh about him missing supper.

But for some reason, Charlotte still couldn't fall asleep. In fact, the longer she'd lain in bed, the harder it became to close her eyes and relax.

"Probably too much coffee," she muttered to herself, realizing she'd drunk more than usual to settle the gnawing hunger in her stomach. In her experience, the first days of a diet were always the most difficult. It took her body awhile to adjust to eating fewer calories.

To her surprise, Bob didn't seem to be having much trouble so far. Of course, it had only been one day. Still, whenever he'd tried to lose weight in the past, he'd always grumbled about not getting dessert, but he hadn't said a word tonight. That showed her how committed he was to fit into his dad's old uniform. He'd always admired Les so much and tried to follow his example.

She'd regretted that Les had passed away before her children were old enough to know him. He'd been a strong, handsome man with a deep faith in God and a firm belief in the importance of family.

A chill stole over Charlotte as she walked down the hallway, and she could feel a draft coming from somewhere. She wrapped her robe more tightly around her and then looked for the source of the cool night air. It led her into the family room, where she saw the curtains fluttering in both windows.

She enjoyed opening up the house at this time of year to let in the fresh, warm air, but May nights were still cool in Nebraska, and she'd forgotten to close these windows before going to bed.

She walked over to lower the windows and then picked up her Bible off the coffee table. That's when she noticed Lightning curled up asleep in Bob's recliner. Next to the recliner was the box with Les Stevenson's old World War II memorabilia. Bob had been reading some of the letters and cards his dad had sent from overseas. Christopher had even asked to read some of them, intrigued about the war now that he was included in the reenactment.

Charlotte carried her Bible over to the sofa and sat down, tucking her feet under her and drawing a crocheted afghan over her legs. She switched on the table lamp next to her.

Lightning lifted her head at the sudden infusion of light in the dark room and then leapt off the recliner to join Charlotte on the sofa. The cat sniffed the afghan for a few moments before settling into the crook of Charlotte's legs.

"You make a nice, furry heating pad," Charlotte told the cat, reaching over to pet the brown tabby. At the other end of the sofa lay the photo album she'd been looking at earlier in the evening. It was full of old black-and-white photographs of herself as a youngster, as well as photos of her parents. She enjoyed the old memories those photos evoked whenever she looked at the album.

With a contented sigh, Charlotte opened her Bible to the book of Luke and read her mother's favorite passage, Luke 11:33–34: "No one lights a lamp and puts it in a place where it will be hidden, or under a bowl. Instead they put it on its stand, so that those who come in may see the light. Your eye is the lamp of your body. When your eyes are healthy, your whole body also is full of light."

Sometimes when she'd gone to her mother for advice, her mother had told her to "be a lamp." It was a biblical reminder for her to always do good in the world and spread the light of God's love to others. As a teenager, Charlotte hadn't always appreciated that advice, but now that she was older she saw the wisdom of it.

The lamplight cast a soft glow over the room as she settled deeper into the sofa. She could hear the gentle chirping of crickets outside and found herself enjoying the peace and quiet of the night.

After closing her Bible, Charlotte reached for the photo album. She turned to the pages that showed her mother with her USO group. They looked like a playful bunch, all smiling young girls with soft, cascading curls that just touched their shoulders. Her mother wore a light V-neck dress with big shoulder pads, her head tipped back in laughter. Charlotte could almost hear that laugh and found herself smiling as she slowly perused the rest of the photos.

She would meet with the events committee soon to get more details about the dance. Rosemary had told her it would be held on Saturday night after the school's annual alumni banquet, so she could expect a big crowd. The events committee had set a budget for the dance; Charlotte would have money for music, decorations, food, or anything else within the budget to help make it as authentic as possible.

Organizing the dance would be a big job, but she wanted to do it right to honor her mother. As she turned the next page, she gasped, startling Lightning. The cat lifted her head up to look at Charlotte, blinked once, and then snuggled back into the afghan.

Charlotte stared at the photo, realizing she recognized the young woman standing next to her mother. She wondered how she'd missed it when she'd looked at the photo album earlier this evening. The woman was Anita Wilson, a faithful member of Bedford Community Church whom Charlotte enjoyed visiting whenever she had the chance. Anita was full of spunk and had a razor-sharp memory.

She closed the book with a happy smile, knowing that Anita would love giving her suggestions about the USO dance. Anita had been one of her mother's dearest friends and always liked to talk about the old days.

The sound of footsteps on the stairs made both Charlotte and the cat look up. She gently lifted the cat off her legs and then placed her feet on the floor, wondering if one of the kids needed her. A moment later, she saw Sam walk by the doorway.

"Sam," she called out to him.

He stopped, looking surprised to see her there. "Hey, Grandma, I didn't know you were still up."

"I couldn't sleep," she told him, setting the photo album aside. "Are you having the same problem?"

He shrugged. "I'm kinda hungry. I thought I might make myself a sandwich."

Charlotte shook her head, amazed at how much that boy could eat. "I'll make it for you," she offered, rising to her feet.

"I don't want to bother you."

"It's never a bother," she assured him, following Sam into the kitchen.

She walked to the refrigerator and opened the door. "Ham?"

"Of course," he replied, retrieving a plate from the cupboard, "with lots of spicy mustard."

Charlotte knew spicy mustard would keep her up all night, but it didn't seem to bother Sam. She ignored the growling of her own stomach as she slathered mustard on both pieces of bread and then placed a few slices of ham in between them.

"Here you go," she said, handing him the sandwich. "How about a glass of warm milk to go with it? That might help you sleep."

"Gross," he said, giving a little shiver. "I think warm milk would just make me sick. I'll take a glass of *cold* milk though."

"Coming up."

By the time Charlotte poured the glass of milk, Sam had eaten half the sandwich. She set the glass on the table and sat across from him. The two of them didn't get much time alone together, and she knew they'd have even less once he graduated. Her heart contracted at the thought, and she swallowed to relieve the tightness in her throat.

"That hit the spot," Sam said, licking the last of the bread crumbs off his fingers. He took a deep gulp of milk and got up from the table. "I'll just take the rest of this milk upstairs with me."

"Okay," she said, reaching for his empty plate.

"I've got it, Grandma," he told her, taking the plate to the sink and rinsing it off. Then he turned around and looked at her for a long moment.

"Do you want something else?" she asked. "Another sandwich?"

"No thanks. One was enough." He shifted on his feet and then cleared his throat. "I was wondering though..."

His words lingered in the air as she waited for him to continue. Whatever he wanted to ask her must be important to him or he would have just come out with it already.

"What is it, Sam?"

He took a deep breath. "I was wondering if we'll have any graduation announcements left after we send out all the ones on the list."

She and Sam had composed a list before they'd ordered

the announcements, not wanting to spend any more money than necessary. Still, his question surprised her. She couldn't figure out why he seemed so nervous about it.

"We should have a couple of extra," she said at last. "I want to save one for your scrapbook. Did you think of more people you want to invite?"

Sam hesitated. "I wanted to invite . . . my dad."

Charlotte froze. They'd discussed inviting Kevin when they'd first made the list, but Sam hadn't wanted him at his graduation. She wondered what had changed since then.

"I mean, he probably won't even come," Sam continued, "but the way Grandpa was talking about his dad tonight, it just made me wonder . . ."

"Wonder what?"

Sam shrugged, as if not sure of the answer himself. "I don't know. I guess I just wondered if someday I might regret not inviting him to my graduation."

Charlotte was more worried that Sam would have to live with the memory of disappointment if he invited Kevin Slater and his dad was a no-show at his graduation. Kevin had already disappointed the kids so many times in their young lives. She just didn't understand how a parent could hurt his children like that.

"Unless you don't want him to come," Sam said, watching her face.

"Of course he can come," Charlotte said, trying to keep her voice neutral. She didn't want her own negative feelings about Kevin to influence Sam. If he wanted his father at his graduation, she'd make sure he was invited.

"Great." Sam drained the last of his milk and set the glass on the counter. "Good-night, Grandma."

"Good-night, Sam."

After he left the kitchen, Charlotte walked over to the pile of graduation announcements that she planned to address and mail tomorrow. She picked one off the top for Kevin, wondering if she should add a personal note warning him not to disappoint her grandson. But what could she say? *Your son needs you?* If Kevin didn't know that by now, he never would.

She slipped the announcement into one of the envelopes and wrote Kevin's name and address on the front with a request to forward in case he had moved again. This way, if they did run out of announcements, she wouldn't have an excuse not to send him one.

"You have three wonderful children, Kevin," she murmured as she sealed the envelope. "I hope you do something to deserve them someday."

Chapter Five

Charlotte was pleased to see that her clematis vine was still clinging to the mailbox post on Wednesday when she put the stack of graduation invitations inside the box. She'd placed a rubber band around the envelopes to make them easy for Todd to handle.

As she closed the mailbox, Toby came dashing up to her. The dog was a little damp after running through the dew-laden windbreak, one of her favorite morning activities. Charlotte leaned down to pet the dog and carefully checked her head and ears for ticks. This was the prime time of year for those pests, and they loved to lodge themselves in the dog's fur.

Satisfied that Toby was tick-free, Charlotte headed back toward the house. She made a mental note to pick up a flea-and-tick collar when she went to town this afternoon. She'd need some postage stamps too because she'd used up all the stamps she'd had on hand sending out the graduation announcements.

The sound of a tractor made her turn back toward the road, and she was happy to see Pete driving toward her. He'd left for the field before she and Bob had even gotten out of bed this morning, obviously eager to get a good start on the day.

He waved to her as he turned the tractor into the driveway, and she smiled as she waved back. Maybe she had overreacted to his skipping out on supper last night. Now that Pete was married to Dana and living in town, she had to adjust to some things being different. Charlotte was still struggling a little to find her place in Pete's life and kept reminding herself that he had a wife to take care of him now.

Pete slowed the tractor to a halt in front of the fuel tanks and then climbed down to the ground. As she walked toward him, she saw Pete unhook the nozzle on the diesel tank and insert it into the tractor.

"Hey, Mom," he said when Charlotte and Toby reached the tractor.

"Good morning. Looks like you were up before the sun today."

"I have a lot to do."

"Did you have time for breakfast? I could make you some eggs."

"No thanks. I'm good." Pete reached down to pet the dog. "Got any ticks on you, girl?"

"I just checked her," Charlotte told him. "I'm going to pick up a collar for her this afternoon. Do you need anything from town?"

He paused for a moment and then shook his head. "I can't think of anything."

"I suppose that's one of the advantages of living in town," she said. "You can pick up supplies on your way to the farm in the morning or when you're headed back home at night."

"I suppose it is."

Charlotte knew her son well enough to sense something was wrong. He seemed a little distant, as if something were weighing on his mind. She wondered if he were having problems with Dana, but knew it wasn't her place to ask.

If Pete wanted advice, he'd ask her. Even then, she knew she'd have to tread carefully. Charlotte wished she could be more like Ma Mildred, who had seemed to intuitively know the boundaries a mother should have when Bob and Charlotte married and moved to the farm. Even when Charlotte went to her for advice, Ma Mildred had known how to dispense marital wisdom without stepping on any newlywed toes.

"How's the house coming along?" she asked.

He shrugged and then glanced over his shoulder to check the diesel nozzle. "All right, I guess. The builder is waiting on the plumber, so that just means more delays."

"Are you headed back out to the field?" Charlotte asked him, feeling as if she were carrying on a one-sided conversation—which was unusual, since Pete had always liked to talk.

"Yeah."

She struggled to find something else to say, still hoping he'd open up to her. The silence stretched between them until Charlotte remembered the main topic of the family's supper conversation last night.

"You need to keep Memorial Weekend open," she told her son. "We have big plans."

"What kind of plans?"

"Well, I'm sure you're aware that the fire department is sponsoring a World War II reenactment to commemorate our veterans, and your dad is in charge of setting it up. He wants all the Stevenson men to take part."

Before Pete could reply, Bob emerged from the barn, wiping his oily hands on a rag. "Did you finish planting the Home Quarter?"

"Not yet."

"Well, you better get on it. They're predicting rain in the next couple of days."

"Yeah, I know," Pete said sharply. "I have a radio in the tractor cab."

Bob stared at his son for a long moment. "Something bothering you?"

Pete met his gaze. "I'm not going to be able to make it to the war reenactment. I'll be too busy planting short-season corn on the south forty acres of Sawchuck's Quarter."

"What on earth are you talking about?" Bob asked, looking at his son as if he were crazy. "You already planted soybeans there."

"Yeah, I did." The diesel nozzle clicked off, and Pete yanked it from the tractor. "Too bad I didn't know it was a complete waste of time and money because you decided to spray herbicide on that field instead of waiting for me to do it."

Bob's eyes narrowed. "I was trying to you help out."

Pete placed the nozzle back on the diesel tank. "Well, did you happen to look at the herbicide containers when you were filling the tank? Because one of them had pre-emergence *corn* herbicide in it."

Charlotte's heart sank. She knew that as little as a gallon of corn herbicide mixed with soybean herbicide would be enough to keep the soybean seeds from germinating. It was a rare mistake, but it had happened to farmers before. Not only did they lose money, but they also were often embarrassed because the neighboring farmers could see that they'd botched the job.

"I only put soybean herbicide in that tank," Bob explained, growing prickly. "The soybean herbicide is in the yellow containers, and the corn herbicide is in the white containers. Been that way for years."

"Things change, Dad," Pete retorted. "I used an empty soybean herbicide container that I had on hand to hold some corn herbicide that was leftover after I was finished planting corn. I even marked a big red C on the label of the container so I wouldn't forget what was in it."

"How was I supposed to know that?" Bob asked him.

"I could have told you if you hadn't decided I wasn't moving fast enough for you. Instead of asking me how you could help, you just filled up the herbicide tank on your own and headed out to the field."

An angry flush stole over Bob's face, but he didn't say anything.

"I didn't even realize what had happened," Pete continued, "until I was in Sawchuck's and checked the south forty yesterday. I'd been wondering why the crop wasn't coming up. When I dug down in the soil and saw the seeds all shriveled, I had a gut feeling that you'd mixed that leftover corn herbicide in with the soybean herbicide. When I saw the empty container in the barn last night, I knew for sure."

Now Charlotte understood why Pete had peeled out of the driveway last night and started his workday so early this morning. He must have been trying to avoid his father until he got his temper under control. From the expression on her son's face, he hadn't waited long enough.

Bob's face didn't look too good either. The more Pete spoke, the redder it got. Charlotte was afraid his blood pressure was going through the roof. She had to find a way to defuse this situation before it got out of hand.

"Now, Pete," she said calmly, "I know you're upset, but it sounds like it was an accident. You know your dad was only trying to help."

"Well, his *help* just cost me thousands of dollars. I have a house to pay for and a wife to support. I can't afford that kind of help."

"Don't we have crop insurance?" Charlotte asked, all too aware of Bob silently fuming beside her.

"Yes, but that only covers the cost of planting." Pete screwed the gas cap back on the tractor. "We'd lose even more if we didn't have insurance."

"Can't you just replant the soybeans?" she asked. "It's still early in the month."

"Thanks to Dad's *help*," Pete said wryly, "I won't be able to plant another soybean crop there for at least another year. Maybe two."

"You're the one who put the corn herbicide in the wrong container," Bob growled.

"It was the only thing I had on hand at the time," Pete replied. "That's why I marked it. You're the one who taught me never to let anything go to waste."

Bob folded his arms across his chest. "Well, I sure didn't teach you to do something as dumb as putting corn herbicide in a soybean-herbicide container."

Pete's jaw clenched, and Charlotte knew that Bob had said the one word sure to enrage their son.

Dumb.

Pete had been sensitive to it ever since he dropped out of high school, causing people to assume he couldn't handle the schoolwork. He used to fly into rages whenever anyone even insinuated that he wasn't as smart as Bill.

Charlotte could see the argument escalating between them but felt powerless to do anything about it. Even Toby sensed the growing discord, turning tail and heading toward the windbreak to hide.

"Why don't we go into the house and talk about this over a cup of coffee?" Charlotte said at last. "I can make you a sandwich, Pete. You're probably hungry after starting work so early this morning."

"Dana already packed me a lunch," he said, dismissing her offer. "I've got to get back out in the field."

"You can blame me all you want," Bob said, not ready to let the conversation go, "but you never told me about that container. Why didn't you write *corn herbicide* on it instead of the letter C? I didn't even see it on there."

"I was in a hurry," Pete grumbled. "Besides, I do most of the work around here now. I don't have to report everything I do to you."

"And I don't have to pick up the slack when you fall behind," Bob retorted. "I do it because I care about this farm and want to see things done right."

Charlotte closed her eyes, knowing they were both saying things now that would be hard to forgive and forget. She had rarely seen Bob so angry. Charlotte stood between her husband and her son, feeling pulled in both directions.

"You're saying I don't do things right around here?" Pete said. "Aren't you supposed to be retired?"

Charlotte didn't want to hear another word. "That's enough, you two. We're never going to solve anything like this."

"Oh, I'm done," Bob spat out. "You want me to leave you on your own, Pete? You got it. I'm done helping out around here."

Without another word, Bob turned and stalked off toward the house.

"Suits me fine," Pete called out as he climbed into the tractor cab. The engine roared to life, and he took off down the driveway.

Charlotte watched Pete drive away, wondering if it was for the best. Maybe once their tempers cooled, Bob and Pete could make some sort of peace.

But as she walked back to the house, their angry, hurtful words rang in her ears. She sensed that this tension between them had been building for a while now, and she couldn't figure out why. The only thing that had changed recently was Pete's marriage to Dana. Maybe Bob, in his own way, was having as much difficulty navigating this new situation with their son as Charlotte was.

Still, an argument like that wasn't going to resolve anything. Even though she didn't like what they'd said to each other, she could see both sides. Pete had lost a lot of money, so he was naturally upset. On the other hand, Bob had only been trying to help. It was just one of those situations where no one was really at fault.

Unfortunately, Charlotte wasn't sure she could convince either father or son to see it that way. In her mind, the worst part was Pete's refusal to participate in the reenactment. She knew how much that had hurt Bob, even if he hadn't shown it.

At least time was on their side. Memorial Day was more than three weeks away. Surely by that time they would come to their senses and call a truce.

When Charlotte reached the house, she went looking for her husband and found him emerging from their bedroom. She was surprised to see that Bob had changed out of his work clothes already.

"What are you doing?"

"I'm getting ready for my meeting at the fire hall." He walked over to the counter and poured himself a cup of coffee.

She looked at the stove clock, noting that it wasn't even ten o'clock yet. "But that's not until this afternoon."

"I meant what I said out there, Charlotte. If Pete doesn't want my help, then I'll just be a full-time retiree." He set his coffee cup on the kitchen table. "I'm sure I can find something around here to keep me busy."

"Now, Bob, you know this thing between you and Pete will blow over. You were telling me last night how much stress Pete is under with the planting and all the problems he's had with the house he and Dana are building. I'm sure he was just blowing off a little steam today."

"That was more than steam," Bob countered. "He meant every word, and so did I."

Charlotte opened her mouth to say more but changed her mind. She needed to let Bob cool off before bringing up the subject again.

"Anything you want done around the house?"

Charlotte swallowed a sigh. "Emily's bedroom door has been squeaking for a while, and there's a piece of siding that's loose on the east side of the house near the window. I can hear it banging every time the wind blows."

He nodded. "Fine. I'll take care of those things as soon as I finish my coffee."

Charlotte knew those two chores would take him only an hour or so. Then what? The farm was Bob's lifeblood. He'd go crazy spending every day inside the house.

And so would she.

Charlotte could only hope he'd soon grow bored and change his mind about not helping out on the farm anymore.

Chapter Six

Wednesday afternoon, Christopher told Dylan about the World War II reenactment as they walked to Dylan's house after school. They had three full hours to spend together until Sam picked him up after he got off work at the airport.

"What do they do at a reenactment?" Dylan's body twitched as he tried to kick a large pebble in front of him and missed it the first time. When he tried it again the pebble sailed a few feet down the sidewalk.

"I'm not sure exactly," Christopher replied. "I guess they shoot at each other or something."

"Sounds like some people have to pretend to be the Germans."

Christopher shrugged, realizing he should have asked his grandpa more questions about it. "Maybe. We fought the Japanese and the Italians in World War II too. I was reading some of my great-grandpa's letters from the war last night. He sent them from lots of different places, like England, Belgium, and France."

"Sounds like there'll be a lot of people there," Dylan mused, kicking at the pebble again.

"All I know is that I get to be part of it." Christopher puffed his chest out a little. "My grandpa said all the Stevenson men will."

"Maybe you'll get to blow something up. That would be pretty cool."

"We'll probably use pretend bombs or something," Christopher told him. "It would be fun to throw a grenade, even if it was a fake one."

"Yeah, that would be fun." Then Dylan turned to him, a grin spreading across his face. "Hey, I know something we can blow up right now."

"What?"

"Come on! I'll show you."

Dylan broke into a run, his body twitches giving him a strange, galloping motion. Christopher trotted along beside him, eager to see what Dylan had in mind.

A few minutes later they were standing in the Lonetrees' garage. Dylan headed straight to the back, where junk was piled up in boxes.

"Do you have a bomb in there or something?" Christopher asked.

"Better," Dylan replied, digging through the box in front of him. "Fireworks."

Christopher watched him pull out a faded red, white, and blue box and set it on the workbench in front of them. "Where did you get that?"

"My mom went to an estate sale last week, and it was sold with a big box of other junk. She only wanted the yarn in the box so she told me to throw the rest of the stuff away. I found this at the bottom of the box."

Christopher pulled open the lid and saw two paper rockets inside, each with a long fuse coming out of the tail. "What are you going to do with them?"

"Shoot 'em off, of course," Dylan said, retrieving a book of matches from a drawer in the workbench. "I know the perfect place to do it too. No one will even see us."

Christopher hesitated. He was not convinced they could shoot off fireworks without somebody noticing. But Dylan was already on his way out of the garage, the box tucked under his arm.

Christopher followed him into the backyard, where they climbed over a fence. "Where are we going?"

"You'll see." Dylan flashed a grin at him. "Unless you're chicken . . ."

"I just don't want to get caught."

Christopher knew his grandparents wouldn't approve of him shooting off fireworks. Even on the Fourth of July he was only allowed to light sparklers or those little black tablets that grew and slithered like worms when you lit them, but nothing that exploded.

"We won't get caught," Dylan assured him. "I already shot off one of these rockets when I first found them. It just shot up into the air a little way and then popped open into a poof of smoke. I think they're too old to do anything really amazing."

That made Christopher feel a little better. There were only two rockets left, after all. And it would be pretty cool to see them fly. He wondered if the paper rocket got shredded into confetti when it popped open.

They reached an empty lot surrounded by overgrown

cedar trees on three sides and a hedge of lilac bushes on the fourth. Dylan walked over to a bare spot in the grass near the hedge and set the box on the ground.

Christopher could see a thin layer of black ash on top of the dirt. "Is this where you shot off the other rocket?"

"Yep." Dylan pulled the book of matches out of his pocket. "You get one of the rockets out."

Christopher opened the box and retrieved a paper rocket. It was so old the paper crackled as he set it on the ground in front of Dylan.

He watched Dylan strike the match and then touch the flame to the long string fuse. Both boys moved back a few feet as the flame burned its way along the fuse to the base of the rocket.

"Watch this," Dylan said, his shoulders contorting with excitement.

But nothing happened. The flame flickered, and the rocket just sat on the dirt launching pad. The boys waited for several minutes; finally Dylan walked over to the paper rocket and kicked it over.

"Looks like this one's a dud," Dylan said.

"It's probably too old."

"Yeah, probably." Dylan got the other paper rocket out of the box. "I hope this one works."

Christopher did too. Since they'd come all this way, he wanted to see at least one rocket blast off.

Dylan's arm kept twitching as he tried to light the fuse, causing the match to go out.

Christopher walked over to him. "Can I try it?"

"I guess." Dylan handed the matches to him.

Christopher struck a match and held the flame against the fuse. It took hold right away, and the boys quickly backed away from the rocket.

A moment later it shot straight into the air, leaving a trail of gray smoke behind it.

"Cool!" Christopher exclaimed.

The rocket arced and whistled; then it began spinning crazily through the air. It flew over the lilac hedge and out of sight.

The boys raced over to the hedge, pushing through the leafy branches to the other side. Christopher realized they were in someone's backyard and saw a plume of smoke rising from a rosebush. The squeak of a door opening made him look up at the brick house, and he saw an elderly man emerge.

"Hey, you boys," the man shouted, shaking his cane at them. "Get over here!"

Christopher froze. "What do we do?"

Dylan didn't hesitate. "Run!"

They turned and dashed back through the hedge. Both boys were out of breath by the time they reached the Lonetrees' garage.

"Who was that?" Christopher gasped.

"Old Man Kimball." Dylan closed the garage door. "I've never met him before, but he pays my stepdad to mow his lawn once in a while. He looks like a real grouch."

Light filtered in through the dusty garage window; Christopher walked over to it and peered through the glass. "I don't think he followed us."

"No, we lost him," Dylan said. "The guy looks like he's

a hundred years old, so he probably can't move very fast. Especially with that cane."

"Does he know who you are?"

"Nope. I've never been over there before, so I think we're safe."

Christopher breathed a sigh of relief. "He looked pretty mad."

"Probably because we bombed his rosebush."

Christopher emitted a nervous giggle, unable to help himself. "Yeah, that wasn't good, was it?"

"Maybe we should stay in the house until your brother picks you up."

"Good idea," Christopher said, following him through the door that attached the garage to the house. He'd had enough of blowing things up for one day.

EMILY WALKED INTO Filly's Flower Shop. She had just enough time to buy the plants and seeds she needed for her organic victory garden before Troy picked her up out front.

They had a date at Jenny's Creamery for ice cream as soon as he was done with track practice. Emily had walked from the high school and was eager to see what kind of selection Filly had in stock. She always carried vegetable plants and seeds in the spring, as well as flowers.

The shop was empty, but she could hear someone talking in the back room. It sounded as if Filly were on the telephone, so Emily walked over to the carousel display of flower and vegetable seed packets and began looking them over.

It was too late in the season to plant carrots, potatoes, or onions, but she had lots of other vegetables to choose from. She wondered what kind of vegetables her great-grandmothers had planted in their victory gardens during the war and found herself wishing she'd asked Grandma and Grandpa before she'd started shopping.

"Hello," Filly said, walking toward her. "Sorry I couldn't help you sooner; I was taking a phone order. May is one of our busiest months. It really keeps me hopping."

"That's okay." Emily picked out some strawberry seedlings and set them by the counter. "I'm still looking."

"Well, if you need anything, just give a holler. I'll be in the back room working on some floral arrangements."

"Thanks," Emily said, reaching for a packet of cucumber seeds. A few moments later, she grabbed some zucchini seeds and spinach seeds as well.

The front door of the shop opened, and Emily turned around to see Nicole and Lily walk inside. She swallowed a groan as she turned back to the carousel, hoping Nicole would ignore her.

No such luck.

"Hi, Emily," Nicole said, walking up to her. "What are you doing?"

Emily kept her gaze on the carousel as she slowly turned it. "Buying some plants and seeds for my garden."

"Ewww, spinach." Nicole turned up her nose when she saw one of the seed packets in Emily's hands. "How can you eat that stuff?"

"She's a vegetarian," Lily reminded her, looking uncomfortable with Nicole's behavior.

"So she likes all that green, leafy stuff that gets stuck in your teeth." Nicole moved closer to Emily, a look of concern on her face. "I think you have something stuck in your teeth right now."

Emily wasn't about to take the bait. "My teeth are fine, thanks."

"Well, we'd love to stand here and talk about vegetables, but I have to pick out a corsage for prom. Are you going this year?"

"No," Emily said, growing impatient. She just wanted Nicole to leave her alone so she could pick out her vegetable seeds. Was that too much to ask?

"Gee, that's too bad," Nicole replied. "Nobody asked you last year either, did they?"

"Don't you have a corsage to order?" Emily reminded her.

"Oh, that's right," Nicole said. "I *had* picked out red roses weeks ago for this gorgeous black prom dress I bought in Lincoln. But I found an even *better* dress in Grand Island last weekend. It's this beautiful coral-pink color, so red roses just won't do."

"What a nightmare for you," Emily said wryly.

"My prom dress is made out of this awesome silver material," Lily offered. "It really shimmers when I move."

"Wait until you see her dance in it," Nicole told Emily and then covered her mouth with her hand. "Oops. You won't be there, will you?"

Emily had heard enough. She hadn't thought much about attending the prom this year since she was only a sophomore, but the way Nicole was rubbing it in really made her angry.

Emily grabbed some more seed packets, barely aware of which ones she'd picked out. "I'd love to stay and chat some more, but my *boyfriend* is picking me up for a date at Jenny's Creamery."

"Sweet," Nicole said. "Just like junior high."

Emily ignored her, quickly paying for her plants and seed packets and then walking out of Filly's before she exploded.

Chapter Seven

"I absolutely cannot stand her," Emily announced as she climbed into Troy's black truck.

"Let me guess," Troy said. "Nicole Evans?"

"Yes. She's just so, so, so . . ." She struggled to find the right word. Nicole had been a pain in her side ever since she'd moved to Bedford.

"Annoying?" Troy ventured.

"With a capital A," she huffed. "And rude. And immature. And just plain mean! I don't know how Lily can stand hanging around with her."

"What did Nicole do this time?" he asked her, his hands resting on the steering wheel.

She shook her head. "I'll tell you later. I need a chocolate malt first."

Emily leaned back against the seat and took a deep, calming breath. She didn't intend to let Nicole ruin her date with Troy.

He cleared his throat. "About that . . . I have some good news and some bad news. Which do you want to hear first?"

Emily turned to look at him, her heart sinking. She didn't want anything but good news after her encounter with Nicole. "Please tell me we're still going to Jenny's Creamery."

He winced. "Sorry. I have to go in to work. In fact..." He glanced at his watch. "I'll be late if I don't leave in the next few minutes."

"Oh, no," Emily groaned. She'd been looking forward to their date all day. "Do they really need you tonight?"

"Yeah, I'm afraid so."

Troy had recently been hired as a dishwasher at a steakhouse in Harding, so Emily knew he couldn't very well call in sick. Still, he seemed awfully cheerful for a guy who was standing her up.

Curious, she asked, "So what's the good news?"

"Well, first, why don't you tell me what you're doing on the Saturday night after this one?"

She shrugged. "I don't know. I'll probably go to the promenade with Ashley. We want to see all the different prom dresses."

The promenade allowed members of the community to see all the prom couples and take pictures before the dance began. Emily had gone with her grandma last year to see Sam and Arielle and take their picture. This year, Arielle's parents had offered to take pictures for both families.

"Well," Troy said with a slow smile, "how would you like to be *in* the promenade instead of just watching it?"

She stared at him for a long moment, feeling a nervous tingle in her stomach. "What do you mean?"

"I'm asking you to the prom, Emily. It turns out I don't have to work that Saturday night as long as I work every weeknight for the next couple of weeks."

"Troy!" she exclaimed and then leaned over to give him

a hug. "Why didn't you tell me right away? Oh, my gosh! I don't believe it. Ashley won't believe it either."

Neither would Nicole. She couldn't wait to rub it in her smug face.

His smile widened. "Does this mean you'll go with me?"

"Of course I'll go with you," she replied, giving him a playful punch on the arm. "How could you ever doubt it?"

"Well, it's really short notice," he reminded her. "I mean, the prom is only about ten days away. Will that give you enough time to get a dress and stuff?"

"I've got plenty of time to find a dress," she said, waving away that obstacle.

Despite her excitement, Emily knew it wouldn't be that easy. With all her schoolwork, she didn't really have time to sew a prom dress and didn't have enough money to buy one either. She hoped Sam might give her a loan, or even Grandma.

Then there were her hair and her nails. She could do her own nails, but she'd need help with her hair. Most of the girls going to prom had made hair appointments weeks ago at the Cut-and-Curl salon. Still, it wouldn't hurt to call to see if Arleta could squeeze her in. She'd need money for that too. And she'd need a backup plan in case Arleta was booked solid. Maybe Ashley or Dana could do her hair, especially if she found a cute updo style on the Internet they could copy.

"Earth to Emily."

She blinked, realizing she'd zoned out of her conversation with Troy. "Sorry," she said, laughing. "I guess I was thinking of everything I have to do."

"Are you sure it's not too much?" he asked, looking a

little concerned. "We don't have to go to the prom. We could do something else that night."

He had to be kidding.

"We're going to the prom," she said firmly.

"Okay," he said, placing his hand on the ignition. "Do you want me to drive you home?"

"No, that's okay," she replied, unlatching her seat belt and reaching for the door handle. "I'll call Sam and have him pick me up in town after he gets off work. There's something I need to do."

"All right." Troy started the pickup, revving the engine a few times. "See you later."

Emily climbed out of the truck, waving to him as he drove off. Then she turned and walked back into Filly's Flower Shop.

"Back so soon," Nicole said when she saw her. "Did you forget some seeds? I hear cabbage is especially good for constipation."

Lily stepped away from her friend as Filly emerged from the back room holding three white calla lilies.

"Hello, Emily," Filly greeted her. "Did you forget something?"

Emily walked up to the counter, ignoring the snickering Nicole. "Actually, I did. I need to order a corsage and a boutonniere for the prom."

"You're going to the prom?" Nicole said with a snort. "Since when?"

Emily turned around. "Since Troy asked me. It turns out he doesn't have to work that Saturday so we're going together."

"I'll believe it when I see it," Nicole replied, rolling her eyes.

"Well, you'll see it next Saturday night," Emily told her. "Or rather, you'll see *me*. I'll be too busy having fun to notice you."

"Now girls," Filly said, "why can't you just be happy for each other? It sounds like you'll all get to have fun at the prom this year."

"You're right, Filly," Nicole said primly. "We should be happy that Emily doesn't have to sit home alone this year. What color is your prom dress, Emily?"

"You'll just have to wait until prom night to find out." Then she turned back toward the counter. "May I look at a sample book?"

"Of course, dear," Filly said, reaching under the counter to retrieve another album. "I recommend you go with roses, since I will have plenty of those in stock in all different colors."

"Roses are fine," Emily told her, opening the album. She'd wear dandelions as long as it meant she was going to the prom. "Although, I'm not sure what color to get."

She could hear Nicole and Lily whispering behind her, but she couldn't make out their words. Emily tried to ignore them as she looked at the pictures of corsages and boutonnieres in the album. At last she pointed to a spray of light pink roses, knowing that shade of pink would go with almost any color of dress except red.

"I'll take this one."

"Good choice," Filly said with a smile. "I'll have it ready for you by the Friday afternoon before prom. You can pick them up then or on Saturday morning."

"Thank you," Emily said, reaching for her purse. It suddenly occurred to her that she might not have enough cash to pay for the flowers. She pulled out her billfold and then peered inside. "Um . . . I'm not sure . . ."

"You can pay me when you pick them up," Filly said with a wink.

Emily breathed a silent sigh of relief. "Thanks, I will."

Then she turned and walked out of the shop, giving Nicole a little wave. "Bye. See you at the prom."

"BUT WHY CAN'T I GO?" Emily wailed, looking in disbelief at her grandmother.

Charlotte stood at the kitchen sink, washing the supper dishes. Emily was supposed to be drying, but she'd dropped the dishtowel on the counter as soon as Charlotte had nixed her plan to go to the prom.

"You're too young," Charlotte told her. "You can go next year when you're a junior."

"But I want to go this year." Emily's lower lip began to tremble. "Please, Grandma. Please!"

Charlotte steeled herself against the tearful pleas. Emily had come home this afternoon on cloud nine, announcing that Troy had asked her to the prom. She apparently hadn't heard Charlotte say that she'd need to talk about it with Bob. Now the news that Emily wasn't allowed to go to the prom seemed to come as a complete shock to the girl.

"Emily, you weren't even talking about the prom twenty-four hours ago. Why the sudden desperation to go now?"

"I *always* wanted to go," she insisted. "I just didn't think it was possible because Troy has to work in Harding on the weekends."

"Well, I'm sorry, Emily, but your grandpa and I have made our decision. You and Troy can go to the USO dance instead."

"I don't want to go to the USO dance. I want to go to the prom." Tears filled her eyes. "This is so unfair. It's like you want me to be miserable."

"Now, Emily," Charlotte said softly. "You know that's not true."

"It *is* true," she said petulantly. "I already told Troy I was going to the prom with him. And I told Ashley and Lily and Nicole."

Charlotte ran the soapy dishrag around a bowl. "Nicole? Why would you tell her?"

Emily picked up the towel, her expression hardening. "Because she was in Filly's today when I was there picking out plants and seed packets. She was really rubbing it in about going to the prom. You know how she is."

Charlotte did know. Nicole Evans and Emily mixed about as well as oil and water. The two girls seemed to bring out the worst in each other.

"So when Troy asked me," Emily continued, "I went back into Filly's to order prom flowers . . ."

"Oh, Emily," Charlotte interjected. "You ordered flowers already? You'll have to call Filly's tomorrow and cancel your order right away. Hopefully, it won't be too late."

"But you *have* to let me go to the prom," Emily cried. "I can't stay home after I told Nicole I was going to be there."

"I'm sorry," Charlotte said, hating to see her hurt like this. "I know how you feel, but Nicole isn't the basis of our decisions around here. Your grandpa and I only try to do what we think is best for you."

"So it's best for me to be a laughingstock?"

"This too shall pass," Charlotte told her.

"I hate when you say that." Emily tossed the towel back onto the counter and stomped out of the kitchen.

Charlotte sighed, wondering if she should go after Emily, and then decided to let her be. She knew how disappointed Emily was and didn't really blame her for feeling that way.

She was so tempted to give in and let Emily go to the prom, but what kind of precedent would that set? Emily was too young, and the prom simply cost too much money. Charlotte was a little irritated with Troy too for asking her at the last minute. She knew it wasn't really his fault, but all this drama could have been avoided if they'd had this discussion a month before the prom instead of only ten days.

As she rinsed the last plate under the tap water, Charlotte wondered what was happening to her family. Bob and Pete were angry with each other, and now Emily was mad at her. The battle lines had been drawn, but she was ready for everyone to call a truce and come together again.

"Lord, help us," she prayed.

Chapter Eight

By Thursday, things around the Stevenson place hadn't gotten any better.

"Emily's still begging us to let her go to the prom," Charlotte told Hannah as they walked along the country road. She'd already filled her in on the ongoing conflict between Bob and Pete. "Do you think we're being too hard on her?"

"I think she's just disappointed. You know how teenage girls are, down in the depths of despair one day and flying sky-high the next."

"I suppose you're right," Charlotte said. "But I'm getting really tired of the depths of despair. Emily keeps naming all the other sophomore girls who are going to the prom and asking for the real reason she can't go."

Hannah smiled. "Sounds like typical teenage warfare. *All the other kids get to do it.*"

Charlotte sighed, realizing she was right. "I believe Bob and I made the right decision, but it's hard to see her hurting like this."

"I know it is." Hannah sympathized. "She'll cheer up eventually; you'll see."

Charlotte unzipped her fleece jacket as the morning sun broke through the clouds. It had been a brisk day when they started out, but it was quickly growing warmer.

"Now, how can I cheer you up?" Hannah asked her.

Charlotte laughed. "Is my mood that obvious?"

Hannah laughed with her. "Only because I know you so well."

"You can help me think of a graduation present for Sam. We can't spend too much money, of course, but I'd like to give him something special."

"Has he mentioned anything he wants?"

Charlotte shook her head. "To tell you the truth, I think the only thing he really wants is for Kevin Slater to come to his graduation."

"Any chance of that happening?"

"I don't have any idea."

"Well, I hope he does come, for Sam's sake. By the way, I'd like to make Sam's graduation cake, if you don't mind. It will be part of our gift to him."

Charlotte didn't mind at all, especially since Hannah did such a beautiful job decorating cakes. "That would be wonderful and one less thing for me to worry about."

"So how do you feel about Kevin coming to Sam's graduation?"

"Honestly? I'd rather he just stayed away. Graduation day is going to be tough enough on me without worrying how his presence will affect the kids."

"The worst part is that Kevin will affect them whether he shows up or not."

"I know," Charlotte agreed. "So I guess I'll just have to take what comes and be a lamp."

Hannah stopped on the road. "Be a what?"

Charlotte laughed at her reaction. "A lamp. It's what my mother used to say to me."

Hannah laughed now too. "Oh, I thought you said be a *lamb*. You know, like Christopher's lamb, Magic."

Now that Charlotte had started laughing, she couldn't stop. It felt good to laugh like that after trying to deal with Emily's drama and the conflict between Bob and Pete. She thanked God that she had a friend like Hannah.

"So tell me why your mother wanted you to be a lamp," Hannah asked more seriously.

"She didn't mean it literally," Charlotte explained. "It was just her way of saying that I should let God's light shine through me and trust in Him to lead the way in times of darkness."

"Interesting," Hannah mused. "It reminds me of that Sunday school song. Do you know the one I mean?"

"'This Little Light of Mine'?" Charlotte ventured.

"That's it."

"This little light of mine, I'm gonna let it shine," Hannah crooned in her lovely alto voice. "I love it when the kids sing that in church."

"So do I. And thank you for cheering me up. I do feel better now."

"Glad I could help. If you find yourself falling into the depths of despair again, just call me up and I'll sing that song to you some more."

Charlotte chuckled, imagining the look on Frank's face if Hannah started singing into the phone. "It's a deal."

"CHRISTOPHER SLATER," Miss Walker said, pointing to him from the front of the class, "please go to the principal's office."

The class made an "ooooh" sound in unison as their eyes all fell on Christopher. Miss Walker, a substitute teacher, clapped her hands together to get their attention.

"All right, everyone, back to work."

Miss Walker had never substituted for his class before, and she was very strict. Obviously, strict enough to send students to the principal just for whispering. He didn't understand why he was the only one in trouble though. Liza Cummings had been whispering to her friends all morning.

Christopher slowly stood up, annoyed that he was being singled out. He'd been sitting at his desk, doing his work and paying attention to the teacher. He'd whispered something to Dylan once or twice, but he was almost sure the teacher hadn't seen or heard him.

"Good luck," Dylan mouthed as he walked past him.

Christopher walked out into the hallway and then turned toward the office. Principal Harding seemed nice enough, but he could be scary too. He had a very deep voice, and it really boomed if he saw you do something you shouldn't be doing.

When Christopher reached the office, he hesitated a moment and then opened the door, ready to face the music.

"There you are," Miss Grienke said. "Alex and Tanya were here five minutes ago." The school secretary motioned to the students seated in the chairs across from her desk. Alex was a fourth grader and Tanya was in fifth grade. Now he was really confused.

"Principal Harding is waiting for you," she said, waving the other two students to their feet. "Go on in."

Christopher followed the other kids into the principal's office, suddenly feeling much better. Maybe he wasn't in trouble after all. He still had no idea why he was here, but Adam and Tanya didn't seem scared at all.

"Good morning," Principal Harding greeted them as they walked through the open door of his office. "Two of you can have a seat while I round up another chair."

Christopher knew that as a sixth grader he could pull rank and take whichever chair he wanted, but he let the others sit down, still uncertain why they were here.

A moment later, Principal Harding brought a third chair into his office. "There you go, Christopher."

Christopher sat down while the principal resumed his seat. Then he folded his hands together and smiled at all three of them.

"I'm sure you're wondering why I asked you to come here today."

Christopher nodded along with Adam and Tanya.

"Well, I'm happy to tell you that the three of you have been chosen by your teachers to write an article for the Memorial Day edition of the school newspaper."

"But school will be out by then," Christopher told him.

The principal smiled. "Yes, I know. I'm sure you're all

looking forward to summer vacation, but this is a very special opportunity. There's going to be a World War II reenactment on Memorial Day, along with some other activities commemorating our veterans. The events committee asked the high school if the students would create a special newspaper for the occasion."

"But we're not in high school," Tanya said.

"I know that too," the principal replied. "The journalism class invited the elementary school to contribute three articles." He shuffled some papers on his desk and then withdrew three sheets of paper. "Here are your assignments. They'll be due in two weeks."

Christopher looked at his assignment on the list of stories. "World War II Veteran Interview," he mumbled to himself, reading the story title under the "sixth grade" heading. "Interview Mr. George Kimball of 2230 Locust Street. He fought in France during the war, and your interview should tell the reader what life was like for him as a soldier."

He stared at the name, wondering if he was having a nightmare. George Kimball? *Old Man Kimball?* This couldn't be right. There had to be a mistake. He couldn't interview Old Man Kimball now—or ever.

"Now for the best part," the principal said, unaware of Christopher's impending meltdown. "You also will read your stories aloud at the war reenactment on Memorial Day, so that's your incentive to do a good job."

Christopher barely heard him, still reeling from his assignment.

"I want you to turn in your interview questions for me to review one week from today," Principal Harding told them. "Then you can contact your veteran and arrange a time to meet for your interview."

"Clyde Deacon is my great-uncle," Adam said, grinning from ear to ear at his assigned veteran. "This is so cool."

"I'm sure you'll all have fun with your stories," the principal said, rising to his feet, "and you'll do the elementary school proud."

As Christopher left the office, he hurried to catch up with Alex and Tanya. "Hey, do either of you guys want to trade veterans? I've got a really cool one named George Kimball."

"No way," Alex said. "I want to interview my great-uncle Clyde."

"I don't want to trade either," Tanya told him. "Mr. Beck goes to my church, so it will be easy to set up an interview with him."

They disappeared into their classrooms, leaving Christopher with no other options.

"What happened?" Dylan asked him when he returned to class. "Did you get in trouble?"

"Worse," Christopher grumbled. "I have to interview a World War II veteran and write a story about it for the high school newspaper."

Dylan's neck twitched as the lunch bell rang. "That doesn't sound so bad to me."

"The veteran I have to interview is Old Man Kimball."

Dylan's eyes widened in horror. "That *is* bad. Maybe you'll get lucky and break your arm or something so you won't be able to write the story."

"Maybe," Christopher said, not feeling very optimistic. "All I know is that I have to find some way to get out of it."

Chapter Nine

"So what am I going to do?"

Emily sat at the lunch table across from Ashley, her stomach too twisted in knots to touch her peanut butter sandwich and baby carrots. Thursday was hamburger day, a favorite among the students, so Emily was one of the few who had brought her lunch from home.

"I guess you'll have to tell Troy you can't go to the prom."

"Shhh," Emily admonished her. "Please keep your voice down. I really don't want everybody in school to know about this."

Everybody was defined as Nicole Evans, who sat two tables away. She was talking to a group of boys, naturally, and her irritating laugh carried all through the cafeteria.

Emily's cheeks flamed. She could just imagine what Nicole would say when she found out Emily wasn't going to the prom after all, especially when Emily had made such a big show about it at Filly's. It made her feel so sick she wrapped up her sandwich and stuffed it into her paper sack.

Ashley leaned closer and spoke in a soft voice. "I hate to tell you this, Em, but they're going to find out eventually."

"Maybe not. I might figure out a way to convince Grandma and Grandpa to change their minds. I still have over a week until the prom. Anything can happen."

"You can't wait much longer. What about finding a dress? Jewelry? Shoes? Not to mention finding someone to style your hair."

"I thought you could style it for me."

Ashley smiled. "I'm not a professional, but it might be fun to try. Do you want curls or an updo or . . ." Then she rolled her eyes. "Listen to me. I shouldn't even be talking about what hairstyle you want for the prom until we figure out how to get you there."

"That's the hard part. There's really no good reason why I can't go to the prom."

"Not according to your grandparents, apparently." Ashley dipped a french fry into the pool of ketchup on her plate. "Do you sense them wavering at all?"

Emily shrugged. "I can't tell. Grandma says she understands how I feel, but she still won't let me go. I've offered to do extra chores around the house, and I promised to be home from the prom by midnight, but nothing seems to sway her."

Ashley motioned toward Emily's lunch sack. "Well, you've got a good start on a hunger strike since you didn't eat a bite of your lunch. Maybe that will soften them up."

"Very funny. I'd do it if I thought it would actually work. Too bad my grandpa's been on a diet, and it's making him grouchier than usual. Something happened between him and Uncle Pete too, but nobody is talking about it. He's so grouchy he won't even listen to all the reasons I should be able to go to the prom."

"Then it sounds like you'll have to wear down your grandma instead."

"Easier said than done." She was about to ask Ashley for a french fry when her friend popped the last one into her mouth.

"I wish I knew what to tell you, Em. It seems like a lost cause."

"There has to be something I can do." Emily wished she could think of the right words to sway her grandma. Didn't Grandma remember what it was like when she was sixteen?

"Your boyfriend is coming this way," Ashley warned, looking past Emily's shoulder. "You'd better tell him what's going on before he forks out a bunch of money."

"I will," Emily said in a hushed voice. "Just give me some time."

Before Ashley could reply, Troy set his lunch tray on the table and then sat on the bench next to Emily.

"Thanks for saving me a seat," he told her, picking up his hamburger with both hands. "I didn't think we were ever going to get out of shop class."

"Can I steal a french fry?" Emily asked him.

"Sure." He pushed his tray closer to her. "Are you finished eating already?"

"Yes. I just wasn't in the mood for a peanut butter sandwich today."

"Do you mind if I eat it?"

"Be my guest." Emily pulled the sandwich out of her lunch sack and handed it to him. "I have some baby carrots too, if you want them."

"No thanks," Troy replied. "I don't want to fill up on carrots before I eat the good stuff."

She watched him take another bite out of his burger and

then felt Ashley's gaze on her. Emily turned to look at her; Ashley mouthed the words, *Tell him.*

"Hey," Troy said, "I'm going to stop by the tux shop on my way to work tonight and pick one out. My mom said to ask you the color of your dress so I can find a tux to match."

Emily bit her lip, avoiding Ashley's gaze. "Ummm ... maybe a black tux and a silver-gray tie and vest."

It was a safe choice, guaranteed to go with almost any dress she could find. *If* she was allowed to find a prom dress, that is.

"Sounds good." Troy finished the last of his burger and then reached for the peanut butter sandwich.

Ashley looked over at Troy. "Don't you have to put down a deposit when you order a tux?"

He nodded. "Yeah, it's like fifty bucks or something, just for the deposit. The rental costs over a hundred."

"That's a lot of money for something you can only wear for one night." Ashley kicked Emily under the table.

"Ouch," Emily said, reaching down to rub her shin.

Tell him, Ashley mouthed to her again as she got up to leave the table.

I will, Emily mouthed back.

Ashley picked up her lunch tray. "Well, I need to stop by the library before my next class, so I guess I'll see you guys later."

"Bye," Emily told her.

Troy waved a french fry at her. "Later, Ashley."

As she watched Troy finish his lunch, Emily wrestled with whether to tell him that she might not be able to go to the prom. If she waited any longer, he risked losing fifty dollars on a tux deposit.

"We're going to have the best time at the prom," Troy said before she could work up the courage. "I might even be able to borrow my cousin's red convertible. Wouldn't that be awesome? We could really arrive in style."

"Troy," she began.

"Or we could ride in a limo," he interjected. "Dave Duval rented a ten-passenger limo and is looking for one more couple to go in on it with him. What do you think?"

"I think there might be a problem."

He turned to look at her, his brow furrowed. "What kind of problem? Are you having trouble finding a dress?"

"No, that's not it. For some crazy reason, my grandparents think I'm too young to go to the prom. I've told them there are some other sophomore girls going, but they're kind of stuck in the past, you know."

His face fell. "Are you serious?"

"I'm afraid so." Emily hated to let him down. "But I'm not ready to give up yet. If I try hard enough, I think I can convince them to let me go."

He gave a slow nod. "Okay. Then I'll go ahead and rent the tux like I planned."

She breathed a sigh of relief, pleased that he had faith in her. "So you won't mind losing the deposit if it ends up that I can't go?"

Troy shrugged. "Well, *I* can still go."

Emily felt as if the floor had just fallen out from underneath her. She'd told Nicole that Troy had invited her to the prom. What would it look like if he showed up with another girl? "So you'd invite someone else to go with you?"

"No way!" Troy replied, looking shocked at the accusation. "I'd go by myself. It wouldn't be as fun without you there, but at least the tux wouldn't go to waste. A bunch of the guys are going stag."

"You'd really go to the prom without me?"

He hesitated. "I guess if you didn't want me to, I wouldn't." Troy picked up his milk carton. "Why don't we just forget the whole thing? I knew it was short notice, and it just seems to be causing problems."

From the other side of the cafeteria, Nicole burst out laughing again. The sound cut through Emily like a knife.

"No, we're not going to forget it," she told him. "You go ahead and rent the tux. I'm going to the prom with you, one way or the other."

AFTER SCHOOL, Sam met Paul and Jake out in the parking lot. He'd been dreading this moment all day and was somewhat relieved that it was finally here.

"Are you guys pumped?" Paul asked, raising his fist in the air. "We're about to pull off a great prank."

"What's the plan?" Jake asked him.

Paul sat on the hood of Sam's car. "This weekend, we'll tow that old Buick out of the pasture and haul it to the school. We'll drop it in the back lot where no one will see it." He turned to Jake. "Did you get the tools?"

Jake nodded. "Yeah, my uncle said we could use them, but he'll need them back by Monday."

"No problem," Paul said. "Between the three of us, we should be able to take that car apart fairly quickly. Then we carry it into the school in pieces small enough to fit through the door."

The more Paul talked, the harder it was for Sam to tell

them what he had to say. Paul seemed really stoked about his idea, and Sam couldn't blame him. It was inspired.

"The car might be easy to take apart," Jake said, "but putting it back together once we're inside the school could be a problem."

Paul shook his head, obviously not sharing Jake's concern. "It doesn't matter. We just need it to look like it's all in one piece. We can hold it together with duct tape if necessary."

"I guess it doesn't have to actually run, does it?" Jake said.

"Nope," Paul replied. "We're just going for the shock value." He looked between Sam and Jake. "Can you imagine the expression on Principal Duncan's face when he sees a full-sized Buick sitting in the hallway right in front of his office?"

Jake grinned. "He's going to freak."

Paul looked over at Sam. "You're not saying much, Slater. Is there a problem with getting a key to the school?"

The time had come. "There's no problem. I'm just not going to do it."

Paul's eyes narrowed. "Why not?"

"Because I refuse to steal the key from my aunt's purse, even if I could find a way to do it."

Paul rolled his eyes. "Like I said before, it's not stealing; it's *borrowing*."

"It doesn't matter what word you put on it; I'm not doing it."

"This prank totally falls apart if we can't get into the school," Jake said. "You're the only way in, Slater. If you bail on us, we're done."

"Look, guys," Sam said, "it's a great idea. I'd be all for it if we didn't have to break into the school to do it."

"If we had a key," Paul reiterated, "we wouldn't have to break in."

Sam shook his head, wondering how to get through to his friends. He'd thought this through long and hard, ever since Paul had first proposed the idea of Sam pilfering Dana's key.

"Here's the deal," Sam told them. "We're not supposed to be in the school on Sunday whether we have a key or not. It might even be a crime. I saw something on the Internet about unlawful entry."

Paul gaped at him. "You looked it up on the Internet?"

"Hey, I'm not going to take the chance of not graduating because of some silly prank." Sam folded his arms across his chest. "I already found out what that feels like last month when I didn't have enough community service hours."

"You really think it would be a crime?" Jake asked. "It's a prank. We're just joking around."

"I know," Sam said. "But the school might not see it that way. I'm not willing to take that chance. Besides..." Sam took a deep breath, finally ready to reveal the most important reason. "I refuse to *borrow* something from Dana without her knowledge. She's my aunt now, and you just don't do things like that, especially to family."

Jake sighed. "Yeah, I guess you're right. It was a great idea though."

Paul still looked dejected, but to Sam's surprise he didn't argue with him any more. He felt bad for letting his friends down, even if he'd done if for the right reasons.

"I did come up with another idea," Sam said, "if you guys still want to pull another prank." He looked between the two of them. "I'll admit it's not as dramatic as a '77

Buick parked in the hallway, but it could be fun. And we'll have our diplomas in our hands by that time, so we won't be in danger of getting caught and missing graduation."

Paul looked puzzled. "Why would we want to play a prank *after* we graduate? I'm not sure how much fun there is in that. None of the seniors will even be in school."

"Not *after* graduation," Sam told him. "During."

"During?" Jake grinned. "That could be fun."

"So what's the prank?" Paul asked, looking a little skeptical.

"Well, you asked me what kind of pranks they did at high school graduations in California. The only one I remember is when somebody in the crowd of graduates started tossing a beach ball around."

"That's not really new or unusual," Paul said. "The only reason you don't see it happening at Bedford is because the principal always checks all the graduation robes right before the seniors go into the auditorium, just to make sure someone isn't hiding something."

Jake nodded. "Last year, he confiscated three cans of silly string and a cowbell."

"We won't be sneaking the beach balls into the auditorium with us," Sam told them. "They'll already be there."

"Where, exactly?" Jake asked.

"In the netting above the stage," Sam replied. "That's where the drama club puts snow and stuff whenever they stage a play. The netting is dark enough that no one will see the beach balls until we pull the lever to release them."

"When do you plan to pull it?" Paul asked.

"Right after we receive our diplomas. All the seniors will be standing on risers on the stage. As soon as the last name is called, down come fifty-two beach balls."

A slow smile spread across Paul's face. "Just imagine

what it will look like when they fall down and start bouncing all over the place."

"Awesome!" Jake exclaimed. "But how can we put them up there without anyone seeing us?"

That was the sticky part. Sam was pretty sure they wouldn't be breaking any laws though, so he was willing to give it a shot.

"We'll head to the boys' locker room after school a few days before graduation," Sam explained, "and just hide out there until everyone leaves."

Paul nodded. "Then we can blow up all the beach balls and place them in the netting above the stage. It shouldn't take us more than an hour."

"That's right," Sam agreed. "We'll have rehearsal the day before graduation, so we'll find out where we'll each be standing on the risers at the end of the ceremony. Whichever one of us is closest to the lever can pull it at the designated time."

Sam waited for a few moments, letting his friends absorb the plan. "What do you think?"

"The idea is growing on me," Paul admitted. "It's fast, cheap, and has a low risk factor."

Jake nodded. "It's growing on me too. I can buy the beach balls when I go to Harding this weekend. I might have to hit more than one store to find fifty-two of them."

"We'll split the cost among the three of us," Sam told him.

"How did you come up with fifty-two beach balls?" Paul asked. "Why not an even fifty?"

Sam was surprised the answer hadn't already occurred to him. "Because we have fifty-two graduates in our class. I want each one of us to have a chance to celebrate by throwing a beach ball around."

Chapter Ten

On Friday afternoon, Charlotte made a visit to Anita Wilson. She parked her car in front of Anita's cute little white bungalow. It had green shutters and rows of pretty yellow tulips on either side of the front porch.

Anita opened the front door as Charlotte walked up the sidewalk. "Hello there," she called out. "You're right on time. I just finished brewing a nice jar of sun tea."

"That sounds wonderful," Charlotte said, stepping over the threshold. "Your house looks so nice."

"Thank you. Most of that is my son's doing. He insisted on fixing things up around here after I fell last autumn and broke my ankle."

"I'm sure it's nice to have a general contractor in the family."

Anita chuckled. "It sure is. Gary put me first on his list and had this place done in a jiffy. Now everything I need is on one floor, even the laundry room."

"So you won't have to climb up and down those basement stairs anymore?"

"Gary told me I'm forbidden from using them unless we have a tornado warning." Anita shook her head. "I'm not sure when he decided he could boss his mother around. I still keep all my potatoes and home-canned goods down there where it's nice and cool."

Charlotte smiled at her independent streak. "Well, just be careful when you go down there. I wouldn't want you to take another tumble."

Anita headed toward the kitchen. "You go ahead and have a seat at the dining-room table while I get our tea. I dug out all my old scrapbooks when you called this morning."

Charlotte set down her bag and walked into the dining room. It was a small room with an antique walnut table and sideboard. A framed family photo hung on the wall opposite the doorway. Charlotte walked over to get a better look at it. In the photograph, Anita was surrounded by her children, grandchildren, and great-grandchildren, a pretty big crew when they all got together.

"Here we go," Anita said as she joined Charlotte in the dining room. "Isn't that a wonderful picture? With the family spread out all over the country, it's hard to get everyone together. My daughter arranged to have this taken during my ninetieth birthday party."

"It's lovely," Charlotte said, taking the glass of iced tea that Anita held out to her.

"Thank you." Anita returned to the kitchen. "Let me grab some gingersnaps, and I'll be right back."

Charlotte turned back to the photograph, wondering if her family would be spread out like that someday too. Sam would be the first to leave, although he seemed so unsure about his future. Maybe that was just part of growing up.

As she took a seat at the table, Charlotte put those thoughts out of her head, remembering the reason she'd come here today.

Anita set a plate of gingersnaps in the center of the table. "I usually try to stay away from sweets, but these give me a nice energy boost in the middle of the day."

Charlotte looked longingly at the cookies but stayed strong. "They look delicious, but Bob and I are dieting."

Anita looked her over. "You don't look like you need to lose any weight to me."

"Thanks, but I put on a few pounds over the winter, so it won't hurt me to cut down a little. Besides, Bob wants to fit into his dad's old war uniform by Memorial Day, so this is my way of lending him moral support."

Anita chuckled as she settled into a chair. "I sacrificed a lot of things for my husband when he was alive, but I never gave up gingersnaps."

Charlotte smiled. "I may sneak one or two before the afternoon is over."

Anita pulled one of the scrapbooks toward her. "I was so excited when you called this morning and told me all about the dance you're planning. It sure took me back a few decades."

"Both you and Mom were in the same USO club, weren't you?"

Anita nodded. "We belonged to the one in Harding. It was very active because one of the main railways connecting the East to the West ran through Harding."

Anita opened the scrapbook. "The soldiers used to come through Harding all the time during the war. Our USO would plan dances and sporting events, anything we thought they might like."

Charlotte scooted her chair closer to Anita so they could both look at the scrapbook.

"The boys were so handsome in their uniforms," Anita said, "and we all had a lot of fun together. I even taught a few of them to dance the jitterbug."

Charlotte looked at the photographs; many of them resembled the ones in her mother's album. "It's nice that everyone could look so happy, even with a war going on."

"I think it was because of the war," Anita told her, growing more solemn now. "Those boys were going across the ocean to fight, and nobody knew if they'd be coming back."

"So you laughed instead of cried?"

Anita nodded. "Most of us had men in our families fighting somewhere too. That's why we treated all the soldiers like family. Each one of those boys was someone's brother or son or sweetheart."

Her words touched Charlotte's heart, and she realized this USO dance should be about more than recreating the food and decorations and dances of the past. It should commemorate the brave spirit of the men and women who came together and faced down the fear and uncertainty that clouded their future.

"Mom used to talk about bringing soldiers home for a home-cooked meal," Charlotte said. "Grandma made a big meal every evening because she never knew how many dinner guests they'd have."

"I did the same." Anita pointed to a photo of a young man in a service uniform. "That's how I met my husband. He was in Harding only for forty-eight hours, but I knew the moment I saw him that we were meant for each other."

"Did he know it too?"

"Maybe not at first, but he answered all the letters I wrote him." Anita breathed a wistful sigh. "Soon he was telling me things about the war that he couldn't tell anyone else. He didn't want his family to worry about him."

Charlotte didn't say anything, aware that Anita was caught up in the past.

"He was wounded in battle and spent four weeks in the hospital there. Then they sent him home, and he asked me to marry him the moment he stepped off the train." She smiled. "We had forty-nine happy years together."

"And a beautiful family," Charlotte said, nodding toward the photograph on the wall.

As the rest of the afternoon wore on, Anita shared more USO stories with Charlotte. She especially enjoyed the stories involving her mother.

"I can't believe Mom actually dressed up like a soldier and tried to sneak onto the train," Charlotte said after one of the more outrageous stories.

"Opal was a pip," Anita said. "It was all to give the boys a good laugh—and it surely did." She looked at Charlotte. "That's the main purpose of the USO: to listen to the soldiers and support them. To keep them smiling."

Her words struck Charlotte in a meaningful way. After hearing all the wonderful stories, Charlotte realized she only needed to concentrate on one goal while planning the USO dance—to keep everyone smiling.

CHARLOTTE PULLED into the farm a little after five o'clock that evening. She'd stopped by Herko's to buy groceries on her way home, stocking up on low-calorie food and snacks. As she parked her car, she saw Bob round the house on the riding lawn mower. He skirted Emily's newly planted garden and headed for the front lawn.

As Charlotte climbed out of her car, she noticed Christopher standing on the corral fence, waving at her.

"Hey, Grandma," he called out. "I want to show you something."

"Okay," she said, opening the back door of her Ford Focus. "Let me take these groceries in, and I'll be right over."

She grabbed two of the bags and headed for the house, her nose itching at the scent of newly cut grass. Just as she reached for the door handle it swung open, and Emily stood on the other side.

"Hi, Grandma," she said cheerfully. "Let me take those sacks for you."

Charlotte made the exchange and then headed back to the car for the rest, pleased at Emily's change in attitude. Only this morning she'd been sad and sullen. Maybe she'd finally accepted the fact that she wouldn't be going to the prom this year.

Emily walked outside and helped Charlotte carry in the rest of the groceries.

"Will you put the milk and orange juice in the fridge for me?" Charlotte asked her, setting her purse on the kitchen table. "I told Christopher I'd be right back out. There's something he wants to show me."

"Sure, Grandma," Emily replied as she set two bags on the kitchen counter.

Charlotte headed toward the barn, noticing for the first time how tall the grass had grown along the border of the corral.

"Over here, Grandma," Christopher shouted to her.

She waded through the grass until she could see him standing in the passageway between the barn and the corral. "What do you want to show me?"

"Watch this," he announced as he stepped out of the barn holding a lead rope attached to a red halter. Magic followed him, seemingly unbothered by the halter he wore. The lamb moved calmly beside Christopher all around the perimeter of the corral until they came full circle to where Charlotte was standing.

"Wow, that's great!" she exclaimed. "Looks like he'll follow you anywhere."

"It took awhile," he confessed. "I finally figured that if I put some alfalfa in my back pocket, he'd follow me trying to eat it. I guess after I did it so many times he finally got used to the halter."

"I'm surprised he didn't chew his way through your pants."

"He only nipped me a few times trying to get to it."

"It's a good thing sheep don't have any upper front teeth," Charlotte said, "or Magic might have taken a bite out of you."

"I know." Christopher turned around to show the half-chewed pockets of his blue jeans. "It just kind of tickled me a little bit."

"Well, just keep working with him. Pretty soon he'll be so tame you'll never need to keep alfalfa in your pockets. Just don't neglect your homework."

Christopher averted his gaze, reaching out to pet Magic's black head. "Okay, Grandma."

"Oh, that reminds me," she told him. "I saw Jim Dickerson at the grocery store. He asked me if you want him to stop over to shear Magic sometime next week."

Christopher pondered the question for a moment "I don't know. Do I?"

"It might be a good idea. Magic's wool is getting pretty long, and the days are growing warmer. He'll be a lot more comfortable if he doesn't have to carry that heavy wool coat around all summer."

Christopher turned to his lamb, an expression of concern on his face. "Will it hurt him?"

"Not at all," Charlotte assured her grandson. "It's just like getting a haircut. Jim does a great job. He and his uncle shear sheep all over the county."

Christopher leaned down in front of his lamb until they were almost nose to nose. "How about it, Magic? Would you like a haircut?"

The lamb started nibbling at Christopher's nose, causing him to back away, laughing. "I'll take that as a yes."

Charlotte smiled. "All right. I'll let Jim know."

As she walked past the house, Bob approached her on the riding lawn mower. When he reached her, he braked to a stop and then cut the motor.

"You can go ahead and start supper," he told her. "I'm almost done here."

She looked at the shaggy areas of grass still left around the barn, as well as the tall weeds growing near the fuel tanks and around the tool shed. "What about the rest of it?"

"That's Pete's concern."

"Oh, Bob," Charlotte said, "how long are you two going to stay mad at each other?"

He looked at her for a long moment. "I'm not mad at Pete. He's made it clear he doesn't need me; so unless that changes, I'll just respect his wishes and keep out of his way."

Charlotte heard the hurt behind his words, even if he didn't express it. She could also see that the farm was going to get a lot more messy-looking without Bob keeping it in shape. Pete just didn't have time for basic upkeep and repairs during planting season. Bob had done that job without ever making a big deal about it. Now she could see how much work he'd actually done.

"See you in a few minutes," Bob said before starting the mower.

Charlotte watched him drive away, sensing that this trouble between her husband and son wasn't going to end anytime soon. At least, not without some help.

She prayed as she walked to the house. "Lord, please knock some sense into these stubborn men of mine. Help them see how much they need each other."

When she reached the kitchen she noticed that all the groceries had been put away. She was about to go find Emily and thank her when the telephone rang.

Charlotte picked it up. "Hello?"

"Hi, Charlotte, this is Dana."

"Well hello, Dana. How are you?"

"Busy," she replied. "This time of year is always a little chaotic at school. I'm sure you're busy preparing for Sam's graduation."

"Among other things," Charlotte said with a chuckle. "I need to make time to go to Harding one of these days and pick up some decorations for his reception."

"I'd love to help you decorate. With everything going on at school, I haven't been able to get out to the farm much lately."

Dana had temporarily taken over the job of the assistant principal, giving her extra duties at Bedford High.

"I'm going to take you up on your offer," Charlotte told her, "but we don't have to wait until graduation to get together. Can you and Pete join us for dinner after church on Sunday?"

"Actually, that's why I'm calling," Dana said. "We're planning to spend Mother's Day with my folks in Grand Island, but Pete and I want to spend some time with you too. We'd like to take you and Bob to supper at Mel's Place tomorrow night if you're free."

"We're free, and we'd love to go out with you."

Charlotte tried to ignore the little stab of disappointment she felt at not spending Mother's Day with Pete. He was married now and had other obligations.

"Wonderful. How about if we meet at Mel's Place about seven o'clock?"

"That sounds fine with me." Charlotte saw Emily walk into the kitchen. "Has Pete said anything about the problem he and Bob are having?"

Dana sighed. "A little. I'm hoping this supper tomorrow night can smooth things out between them."

"I hope so too," Charlotte replied, knowing that would be the best Mother's Day gift she could receive.

When she hung up the phone, Emily was leaning against the counter. "I put the groceries away for you, Grandma."

"I see that," Charlotte said, sensing that there might be an ulterior motive behind Emily's sudden burst of helpfulness. Her granddaughter had spent most of the last couple of days up in her room.

"I've done all my chores already too," Emily continued, "and planted some heirloom tomato plants that Mrs. Givens gave me for my garden."

Charlotte had noticed Emily tending her garden almost every day on the few times she'd come out of her room.

"Why don't we go out and look at it after supper."

"Okay," Emily said, pushing off the counter and heading for the hallway.

"Emily?" Charlotte said before she could leave the room. "Did you tell Troy that you can't go to the prom with him?"

Emily slowly turned around. "I told him that you and Grandpa didn't *want* me to go."

"We're not going to change our minds," she said firmly. "Do I need to call Mrs. Vanderveen and tell her that you won't be going to the prom with Troy?"

A flush stole over Emily's face. "Oh, Grandma, you wouldn't!"

"I won't if you make it clear to Troy that you can't go. It's not fair to him otherwise."

"What about being fair to me?" Emily cried. "You just don't understand. I really, really want to go, Grandma."

"I know you do," Charlotte said softly. "But it's not going to happen this year, and you need to make sure Troy knows that."

"Fine," she snapped, "I'll tell him I can't go."

Emily stomped off to her room, leaving Charlotte in the kitchen alone. She hadn't wanted to threaten her with a call to Mrs. Vanderveen, but she'd had enough of the pleading and crying and buttering up. It only made the situation harder for both of them, especially when Charlotte had no intention of changing her mind.

Chapter Eleven

That evening, Charlotte sat in the family room with Bob and the boys. She was embroidering a pattern of morning glories on a pair of pillowcases and was close to finishing the first one. She wished Emily had joined them, but her granddaughter was still upset with her. Emily hadn't said more than two words during supper and had gone straight up to her room after the Bible reading.

"Listen to this, Grandpa."

Charlotte looked up from her embroidery to see Christopher holding one of Les's old letters in front of him. Her grandson sat beside Bob's recliner; he'd been sifting through the box of Les's war memorabilia.

"Dear Mildred," Christopher began reading. "I hope this finds you well. We're still in England but will be sent out any day now. I'm not sure yet where we'll be going. Some people say we're headed to Holland, but no one really knows. I just hope our company can stay together. I get along well with all the guys here.

"I'm sure you're much busier at home than I am here. Most days we do our drills and then sit around and wait. The chow here isn't too good, so my uniform isn't so snug anymore."

Christopher looked up at Bob, a grin on his face. "See? It sounds like Great-Grandpa Les was on a diet just like you are."

"Humph," Bob grunted. "Except his diet wasn't by choice."

"Keep reading, Christopher," Charlotte said.

"Yeah," Sam said, turning from the computer to look at his little brother. "What else does the letter say?"

Christopher cleared his throat and continued reading. "You probably fed me too much pie before I left home. Not that I'm complaining. I love your pies, and I love you even more."

Christopher looked up from the letter and wrinkled his nose. "Mushy stuff."

"I think it's sweet," Charlotte said, remembering that Les hadn't been a man who showed much affection.

Shaking his head, Christopher started up again where he'd left off. "I hope everything is going well on the farm. Tell Uncle Jack to check the fence in the south pasture before he puts the cows in there. There are a couple of loose posts I didn't have time to fix before I left. And don't forget to keep a good supply of wood by the stove. You know how those big snowstorms can hit in March when you least expect it."

As she listened to Christopher read, Charlotte thought about Ma Mildred being alone on the farm with two young children. Les's uncle had helped out, but she'd been responsible to keep the farm going while Les was gone.

"Write to me as often as you can," Christopher read, "and pray that this war ends soon. Your husband, Les."

Christopher set the letter in his lap, and no one said anything for a long moment. Charlotte couldn't imagine what it would have been like to have Bob fighting in a war halfway around the world while she was alone on the farm with young children. Yet that had been the reality for Ma Mildred and many of the farm families all over the country.

"It's weird," Sam mused. "I thought his letters would be about people he shot in the war and bombs and stuff. It's almost like Great-Grandpa sounds bored."

"Dad didn't talk about the war much," Bob said, "but he did talk about the boredom between battles. He said it was during those times that he got the most homesick."

Christopher looked surprised. "I didn't know adults could get homesick too."

"Sure," Bob said. "My dad had never left Nebraska before he went to basic training. It was the first time he'd ever flown on an airplane too."

"How old was he when he went to the war?" Sam asked.

Bob thought for a moment. "About twenty-three. I was only a baby when he left, so I didn't even know him when he came home from the war." Bob chuckled a little. "Ma said I'd scream whenever he tried to hold me."

"So you were about the same age as I was when my dad left," Christopher said. "Only my dad didn't come back."

Charlotte knew a lot of fathers, brothers, and sons hadn't come back from the war either. That's why it was so important that they honor those who had served their country.

Sam flipped off the computer screen, fully engaged in the conversation now. "What are we going to do during the reenactment, Grandpa? Will we be eating bad chow and doing drills and stuff?"

Bob folded the newspaper and set it aside. "According to the reenactment group from Grand Island, we'll be re-creating a couple of different activities the soldiers were involved in during a specific conflict."

"Do you know which conflict yet?"

Bob nodded. "Most of the Bedford boys, including my dad, were at the Battle of Brittany. They weren't all in the same company, but they fought in the same area of France. So we'll put up tents and dig foxholes like they did to show how they prepared for a night assault."

"That sounds pretty cool," Sam said.

"It sure does," Christopher agreed. "But we won't have to eat the bad chow, will we?"

The question made Bob chuckle. "I don't know yet. Maybe you'd better fill up before we leave that morning."

Sam turned to Charlotte. "Did you order our uniforms, Grandma?"

"I sure did. Rosemary's making some of the uniforms, but she got so overwhelmed with orders that she found a company that makes them. There should be enough uniforms for everybody who wants one."

"Did you order one for Uncle Pete too?" Christopher asked.

Charlotte glanced up at Bob. "No, I don't think Uncle Pete will make it. He's pretty busy this time of the year. But Uncle Bill will be there."

"Oh, that's right." Christopher carefully replaced the letter back in the envelope. "It's too bad Will is too little to be in the reenactment."

Charlotte smiled. "We'll take lots of pictures so Will can see them when he's older." Then she turned to Bob. "How many men have signed up to participate?"

"We've got about eighty so far from all over the county," Bob said. "Paul Hubbard volunteered to let us hold the reenactment on that land he owns that's full of cedar trees. It's not exactly a forest, like where the real battle was fought, but it's the closest thing we have in Bedford."

"I expect all three of you to be at the USO dance on the Saturday night before the reenactment," Charlotte reminded them. "And you'll need to wear your uniforms too."

"Nobody told me I'd have to go to a dance," Sam said. "Will you have good music, or will it be that lame stuff from the past?"

"We'll have good music from the forties," Charlotte told him. "A band from Kearney is coming to play for us; they specialize in the big-band sound."

"Do I have to dance?" Christopher asked.

"No, you don't have to," Charlotte said. "But keep an open mind. There might be a cute girl there who thinks you look pretty handsome in your uniform."

"I hope not!" Christopher exclaimed as his face turned bright red.

Sam laughed. "You can hang out with me and Arielle at the dance, Christopher. We'll keep you safe from the girls."

"Thanks," Christopher said with a sigh of relief as Bob and Charlotte laughed.

They spent the rest of the evening reading more letters and talking about Les's stories from the war. Later in the evening, Charlotte popped a big bowl of popcorn, hoping the buttery aroma would tempt Emily to join them.

As Bob and the boys talked more about the reenactment, Charlotte found herself wishing Pete would change his mind. It just wouldn't be the same without him there.

At the moment, she was more worried about the Mother's Day dinner Dana had planned at Mel's Place tomorrow night. She knew it would be the first time that Bob and Pete had spent more than a few minutes together since their big blowup. She just hoped it didn't turn into World War III.

ON SATURDAY EVENING, Bob parked his truck in front of Mel's Place. The sun was just starting to go down, casting golden sunbeams over Bedford.

"Your tie's a little crooked," Charlotte told Bob.

He looked into the rearview mirror to adjust the tie. "I still don't know why I have to be all dressed up."

"There's nothing wrong with wearing a shirt and tie for dinner out on a Saturday night, especially for Mother's Day."

"Mother's Day isn't until tomorrow."

"I know that, but I'm glad Dana and Pete are taking this time to celebrate with me."

He leaned back in his seat. "I can tell you right now that I'll be the only man in there wearing a tie."

"You look nice. I can tell you've already lost a little weight."

"Only three pounds," he said.

"That's pretty good considering we've been on this diet less than a week." She shook her head. "I don't understand why men can lose weight so much faster than women. I've only lost a pound."

"We probably have more willpower."

As much as Charlotte wanted to argue that point she decided now wasn't the time.

She smoothed the front of her pink silk blouse. "Do I look all right?"

Bob looked her up and down. "You look okay to me."

She plucked a loose thread on her black slacks and then reached for the door handle. "Shall we go in?"

Bob looked down the left side of the street and then the right. "I don't see Pete's or Dana's car here yet."

"They're probably just running a little late. Or maybe they decided to walk from their place. Dana told me that sometimes they like to take a walk together and talk about their day."

She looked over at Bob. "Do you remember when we used to take walks together along Heather Creek?"

"Sure. Maybe we can start doing that again now that I have more time."

His words reminded her that this evening might not go as smoothly as she hoped. She'd been uncertain about whether to bring up the subject today, but now seemed like the perfect moment.

"Bob, there won't be any . . . problems between you and Pete tonight, will there?"

He looked puzzled. "What kind of problems?"

"Well, the last time you two were together you almost bit each other's heads off."

"You worry too much, Charlotte. All of that is settled now."

If by *settled* he meant that Pete only stopped by the house for a minute or two each morning and Bob let the farm fall to pieces around him, then it seemed to her that she did have good reason to worry.

Still, maybe they'd be able to patch up their differences on neutral territory.

When they walked inside Mel's Place, Charlotte looked around for Dana and Pete but didn't see them. "Why don't we sit over there," she said, pointing out a table to Bob.

"Suits me," Bob replied, waving to Dick Barry, who farmed on the other side of Heather Creek Farm.

Charlotte and Bob sat down on the same side of the table. She checked her watch, noting that it was only a few minutes past seven o'clock.

She glanced at the plates on the tables beside them, her mouth starting to water. "I've been so good on my diet today, I don't know whether to have a salad or splurge on something more satisfying."

"That's the willpower I was talking about," Bob said. "It's the splurging that gets a person every time."

Ashley walked up to them holding a pair of menus. "Wow, you two look nice. Are you out on a date tonight?"

Charlotte smiled at Emily's best friend. "We're meeting Dana and Pete for dinner, so we'll wait to order until they get here."

"Okay." Ashley set the menus on the table. "What's Emily doing tonight?"

"She was working in her garden when we left."

To Charlotte's relief, Emily had finally emerged from her room that morning for breakfast but had spent most of the day outside. Charlotte hoped her snit would blow over by the time Monday rolled around.

"I'll bring you some water while you're waiting," Ashley said, "and I'll tell Mom you're here too. I know she'll want to come out and talk to you."

Charlotte looked forward to seeing Mel. They'd both been

too busy to chat much lately. She needed to make more time for her friends, even if life got in the way sometimes.

A few minutes later, Mel emerged from the kitchen wearing a pink apron and a big smile.

Bob scooted his chair back. "I think I'll go over and say hello to Dick while you visit with Mel."

"Okay." She glanced at her watch again, wondering what was keeping Pete and Dana. She hoped Pete wasn't having second thoughts about coming tonight. Surely if that was the case, then Dana would have called to let her know.

"Hello, stranger," Mel said, taking a seat in the empty chair across from Charlotte. "What's new with you?"

"Oh, just the usual," she replied. "Well, maybe not so usual. I've been busy planning the USO–style dance for Memorial Weekend."

Mel smiled. "I've been hearing a lot about that. The dance sounds like so much fun. I'll probably have to work that night, but I'm still going to wear a forties-style outfit."

Charlotte already had one picked out herself. It was a vintage bridesmaid dress that her mother had worn to Anita's wedding in 1945. Her mother had kept it wrapped in plastic at the back of her closet until the day she died. The dress was a simple, knee-length style of the era with the signature shoulder pads and V-neck bodice. The yellow taffeta material might be a little fancy for the dance, but as chair of the dance committee, it wouldn't hurt for her to stand out a little.

"It feels good to get off my feet for a while," Mel said, leaning back in the chair. "We've been hopping tonight. I had to call Ashley in to lend a hand."

"I like your apron. I don't think I've seen that one before."

"Thanks, I bought it from a foundation that raises money to treat breast cancer." She pointed to the pink ribbon on the corner of the apron.

"I'll have to order one too." Charlotte thanked God every day that Mel's breast-cancer treatment had been so successful.

"So what's new with your family?" Mel asked.

Charlotte emitted a tired laugh. "I'm not sure where to begin."

"Problems?"

Charlotte told her about Emily's silent treatment since they told her she couldn't go to the prom, as well as the dispute between Bob and Pete.

"I'm sure Emily will get over it soon," Melody assured her. "She's so excited about that victory garden she's planted. Once the prom's over everything should get back to normal."

Although Charlotte had told herself the same thing, it made her feel better to hear Melody say it too.

"Maybe this thing between Bob and Pete will blow over soon. Ashley told me that he and Dana are meeting you two here for dinner tonight. That's a good first step."

"Except that they're not here yet." Charlotte looked at her watch again. Now it was fifteen minutes past seven.

Then the door opened, and they walked inside.

"It looks like they're here now." Melody rose from the table and greeted them with a smile. "You two have a seat. I'll send Ashley over in a few minutes to take your order."

"I'm so sorry we're late," Dana said as Mel headed back to the kitchen.

"It's my fault," Pete said, taking a chair beside his wife. "I had to pick up some parts in Harding today, and it took me longer than I thought it would."

"That's all right," Charlotte replied. "I'm just glad you're here now. Your dad and I have been having fun visiting with friends."

"Well, I'm starved." Pete slid one of the menus toward himself. "I'm going to order a nice juicy steak."

"That sounds good to me too," Dana said. "What about you, Charlotte?"

Charlotte steeled herself against temptation, remembering Bob's words about willpower. "I'm going to have a salad."

"You have to eat more than that," Pete insisted. "We're treating you tonight for Mother's Day."

She hesitated, knowing it wouldn't take much convincing to change her salad to a steak. "I'm going to wait and see what your father is having."

Pete looked over at Dick Barry's table. "Hey, Dad," he called out, "we're about ready to order over here."

Bob walked back to the table. "Sorry about that. You know how Dick likes to tell a story."

"I sure do," Pete replied. "Did he ever tell you the one about the duck that adopted a litter of kittens?"

As Pete told the story, Charlotte looked between her husband and son, a spark of hope lighting within her. Maybe this dinner would lead to a truce between them after all. They both seemed relaxed and happy. Perhaps she'd been worrying for nothing.

Chapter Twelve

"This is the day that the Lord has made," Pastor Evans proclaimed from the pulpit. "Let us rejoice and be glad in it."

Charlotte sat in the pew next to Christopher, noticing that he had a tiny smear of grape jelly on his khaki pants. The kids had brought Charlotte breakfast in bed this morning to honor her for Mother's Day. They'd also insisted on doing all the cleanup, finishing the job just before it was time to leave for church. She made a mental note to apply stain remover to Christopher's pants as soon as they returned home.

"I'd like to welcome everyone here on this beautiful Sunday morning," Pastor Evans continued, "and wish a happy Mother's Day to all the mothers, grandmothers, and great-grandmothers. Ephesians chapter six, verses one through three tell us: 'Children, obey your parents in the Lord, for this is right. "Honor your father and mother"—which is the first commandment with a promise—"so that it may go well with you and that you may enjoy long life on the earth."'"

Charlotte glanced over at Emily, hoping she was paying attention. Although her granddaughter had pitched in to make breakfast this morning and, with the boys, presented Charlotte with a lovely new embroidery basket, Emily still acted a little aloof.

On this Mother's Day, Charlotte couldn't help but think of Denise. She knew the kids were thinking of her too, and Charlotte wondered if Emily was chafing at obeying her grandparents because she missed her mother.

The sound of the organ broke Charlotte's reverie. She reached for the hymnal and turned to the page listed on the hymn board at the front of the church.

"For the beauty of the earth," she began to sing, sharing the hymn book with Christopher, "for the glory of the skies. For the love which from our birth, over and around us lies. Lord of all, to thee we raise, this our hymn of grateful praise..."

After they finished the hymn, the congregation took their seats once more to listen to the morning's announcements. Charlotte sat up a little straighter, waiting to hear the announcement she'd given the pastor when they arrived at church this morning.

"The monthly meeting of the church board will be held on Wednesday night," Pastor Evans said, "followed by choir practice. The family of James O'Malley will be hosting a birthday party for him at Bedford Gardens next Sunday afternoon. You're all invited to attend. And, last but not least, Charlotte Stevenson has requested a short meeting of the Women's Group after the service today for those able to stay."

"Do we have to stay too, Grandma?" Christopher whispered.

"Yes, but it shouldn't take too long," Charlotte assured

him. "You can wait in the car or hang out with some friends until it's time for us to go."

"Okay," he whispered.

When the service was over, Charlotte did her best to keep the women's meeting short. To her surprise, quite a few of the women made time to hear what she had to say.

"Thank you all for staying," Charlotte told them. "I'm sure many of you have plans today, so I'll try to make this short."

"Don't make it too short," Julia Benson chimed. "My husband forgot where he hid my Mother's Day present, so he and the kids are hurrying home to find it."

Charlotte laughed along with the rest of the group. "Well, I'll try to take just long enough for them to find your present. The reason I called this meeting is because I need some volunteers for the USO dance on Memorial Weekend."

"What do you need us to do?" Julia asked.

"I want a group of women who will re-create a USO group from the 1940s. That means we need to look the part and serve as hostesses for the dance."

"How fun!" Stacie Lindstrom exclaimed. "I'm in."

"Me too," DeeDee Meyer said. "Will we be serving food at the dance?"

That question was one reason why Charlotte had asked for volunteers. She needed help figuring out the details. "I don't know. The dance will be held after the alumni banquet, so everyone will have eaten dinner already."

"What time is the dance?" Lydia Middleton asked.

"It will start at eight o'clock and last until midnight."

"So we'll want to serve something," Lydia said. "People will get hungry again, especially if they're dancing."

"I agree," Charlotte said. "Maybe we should serve a dessert buffet."

"Only if you make your pies," Arlis Bauer said. "Everyone loves them."

Charlotte liked the idea, especially since Ma Mildred had taught her everything she knew about baking pies. Then she remembered the letter from Les about his wife's pies, and that triggered another idea.

"What if everyone brings something special made from a recipe passed down from their mother or grandmother?" Charlotte suggested. "My mother-in-law made pies for her husband before he left for the war. I'm sure there are other family favorites that mothers and wives and sweethearts fed their soldiers."

"My grandmother made kolacky," Celia Potts said. "That was the first thing my uncles asked for when they came home from the war."

As the idea spread among the group, they all began talking about it to each other. Charlotte could tell by the growing enthusiasm that the idea was a hit.

"Does it have to be a dessert?" Nancy Evans asked. "I'd really like to make my mom's chicken and dumplings."

"And I can bring my great-aunt's war bread," Andrea Vink said. "It was a bread recipe she tinkered with because of rationing."

"That does make sense," Charlotte said. "If we want to create authentic World War II recipes, then we need to be mindful about what ingredients were available back then."

"You couldn't just walk into a store and buy as much butter or sugar or meat as you wanted," Lydia told them. "Each family was given a ration book and only allowed a certain amount."

"Then let's improvise, like the women had to do during the war," Charlotte suggested. "They used raisins and other dried fruit to sweeten pies and cakes instead of sugar."

"I mixed boiled turnips in with my mashed potatoes so I had enough to feed my family," Lydia added.

"Are you up to the challenge?" Charlotte asked the group. "We'll make it a potluck instead of a dessert buffet so we have more variety."

"I can't wait to go home and start looking through my mother's old cookbooks," Amanda Hostetler said. "She always wrote down the changes she made to the recipes."

Charlotte was happy to see everyone so excited about the project. "If possible, I'd like everyone who volunteers to be in the USO group to wear clothing from that era."

Nancy raised her hand. "There's a vintage clothing store in Harding called The Good Old Days that rents out clothes from every decade in the twentieth century. I know they'll have a lot to choose from."

"Perfect," Charlotte said. "Are there other ideas for the dance?"

"Why don't we hold a jitterbug contest?" Arlis suggested. "That could add some excitement to the night."

"I haven't danced the jitterbug in so long," Lydia said with a smile. "And I probably shouldn't start again now, but I could be one of the contest judges."

"You're hired," Charlotte told her. "I think a dance

contest is a wonderful idea. I'll ask Anita Wilson to judge too; she used to teach the jitterbug to some of the soldiers. We can make signs about the contest to post around town so people can start preparing."

"I wish I knew *how* to jitterbug," Andrea said.

"Just look on the Internet," Stacie suggested. "There are all kinds of online videos that can teach you almost any dance."

The ideas were flying back and forth, much to Charlotte's delight. The meeting had already gone on twenty minutes longer than she'd intended, and she knew Bob and the kids, as well as the families of the other women, were probably getting impatient.

"All right, I think we've got a good start," Charlotte said. "Before I let you go, I'm going to pass around this sign-up sheet so I know who plans to volunteer. And please invite any friends or neighbors to join our USO group. I think we'll have a lot of fun."

Charlotte watched as almost every woman at the meeting signed the sheet. She couldn't have asked for a better group to help her host the USO dance.

ON MONDAY MORNING, Emily sat in her first-period math class, cramming for the upcoming quiz. She'd worked the practice problems last night, but the concepts hadn't soaked in. She'd been too distracted by the drama going on in her life.

"Good morning, Emily," Mrs. McMurphy, the math teacher, greeted her as she walked into the classroom. "You're here early."

"I wanted to go over my notes one more time before the quiz." She watched the teacher set a stack of folders on her desk. "Is it going to be hard?"

Mrs. McMurphy smiled. "The more you've studied, the easier the test will be. I'm sure you'll do fine."

Emily wasn't so sure. She'd been too depressed about not going to the prom to study this past weekend. Even the silent treatment hadn't worked on Grandma, and she was tired of spending all her time in her room.

At first, she'd kept busy sewing a red, white, and blue sheep blanket for Magic, but that didn't take very long. It was a simple rectangular pattern with elastic bands sewn on the underside corners. All Christopher had to do was lay the blanket over Magic's back and slip each leg through one of the elastic bands.

The rest of the time she'd just listened to music and stared up at the ceiling. At this point, Emily just wanted the stupid prom to be over so she didn't have to think about it anymore.

"Oh no," Mrs. McMurphy said, sifting through the files on her desk.

Emily looked up from her notes. "What's wrong?"

"It looks like I forgot the quizzes at home."

Emily brightened. "Does that mean we don't have to take it today?"

"Sorry," Mrs. McMurphy said as she held up a sheet of paper. "I still have the master copy with me. I'll go make some copies and be right back. Tell the rest of the kids they can have a short study period while I'm gone."

The teacher walked out the door, and a moment later

the first-period bell rang. Students streamed into the classroom.

"Where's Mrs. McMurphy?" Hunter Norris asked.

"She had to make more copies of the quiz," Emily told the other students. "We're supposed to study until she gets back."

Nicole Evans walked into the classroom and took a quick look around; then she walked over to Emily's desk. "Hey, Emily, did you pick out your prom dress yet?"

"No," Emily said, leaning over her notes.

"You'd better hurry," Nicole said. "The prom is this Saturday."

"Thanks," Emily muttered. She flipped a page of her notes, willing Nicole to walk away. There was something in her tone that Emily found more annoying than usual.

"You *are* going, aren't you?" Nicole asked her.

Emily flushed, wondering how much longer Mrs. McMurphy was going to be gone. She looked toward the door and saw Ashley enter the classroom.

"Because I heard a horrible rumor that you made it all up," Nicole continued, "and that you were never even invited to the prom."

Ashley set her books on the desk behind Emily. "She was so invited."

"So she says," Nicole countered. "I'll bet you twenty bucks that she's not at the prom. Want to take me up on that bet, Ashley?"

Ashley slid into her seat. "Don't be stupid."

Emily gave up the pretense of studying and closed her notebook. "Troy and I talked about going to the prom, but we decided it's lame. Why spend all that money for a dress and limo and stuff for just one night?"

Nicole gave her a pitying smile. "That's what all the losers say."

"Sit down and give it a rest, Nicole," Ashley said.

Nicole ignored her. "Well, the party at Dean Wallace's house after the prom won't be lame. His parents are going to be gone for the weekend, and everybody who matters will be there. Troy included."

Emily looked up at her. It was the first she'd heard about a party. "How do you know?"

"Because I was walking by his locker when Dean told him about it. Troy said he wouldn't miss it."

Ashley snorted. "Your parents are letting you go to a party after the prom?"

"I'm staying overnight with Lily on Saturday so they won't know about it. Are you going to tell on me, Miss Goody Two-shoes?"

Ashley gave a small shrug. "I don't really care what you do."

Nicole looked back at Emily. "I'll make sure Troy calls you from the party. There will be a lot of cute girls there, but I'm *sure* you won't have anything to worry about."

Before Emily could reply, the teacher walked back into the classroom, and Nicole hurried over to her own desk.

"Five more minutes to study," Mrs. McMurphy announced.

Emily could feel Ashley's gaze on her, but she didn't look at her. Instead, she opened her notebook and pretended to study, the words blurring on the page. Nicole had just embarrassed her in front of the whole class.

Emily blinked back the tears and took a deep breath. It was bad enough she wasn't allowed to attend the prom; now she was going to be a laughingstock too.

When math class was finally over, Ashley waited for her out in the hall.

"How did you do on the quiz?" Ashley asked her.

"Awful."

"Don't pay any attention to Nicole," Ashley said. "You know how she is."

"I wish I was the one graduating this year so I'd never have to see her again."

"I know."

Emily sagged onto the locker behind her, fresh tears stinging her eyes. "Why did I ever go back into Filly's and tell Nicole and Lily that I was going to the prom?"

"It's not your fault," Ashley consoled her. "You didn't know your grandparents wouldn't let you go."

"I feel like such a loser."

Ashley took a step closer to her. "You're not a loser. Now come on, we're going to be late for history."

"I don't care," Emily said petulantly. "Troy never told me about the party at Dean's house."

"I'm sure he just found out about it. Besides..." Ashley hesitated. "He probably knew you couldn't go and didn't want you to feel bad."

"Too late."

The second-period bell rang, and the hallway started to empty.

"C'mon, Em," Ashley said, heading down the hall. "We don't want to get a tardy."

Emily reluctantly followed her, grateful that Nicole wouldn't be in her next class. "I'm going to Dean's party on Saturday night."

"No way, Em." Ashley started jogging down the hallway toward their classroom. "You would be in *so* much trouble, it's not even funny."

"I won't be in trouble if I'm not caught."

"And how do you intend to make that happen?" Ashley asked when they reached the door.

"I have a plan."

Chapter Thirteen

"My lips are getting tired."

Sam lowered the beach ball from his mouth and looked over at Paul, who sat backstage in the auditorium. "Mine too. How many more do we have to blow up?"

"I'll count," Jake said, sorting through a bunch of balls at his feet. "Three, six, nine, twelve..."

Sam walked over to the curtain and peered into the dark auditorium. They'd been backstage for the last hour. They had realized they needed to do a test run to see if the balls would really be hidden up in the netting. If it looked like their plan would work, they would come back on the last day of classes and put all the balls up above the stage.

"It looks like we have twenty," Jake said at last. "That's enough to do our dry run. We'll wait and inflate the rest when we come back closer to the big day."

Sam finished blowing up the beach ball in his hands and tossed it toward the pile.

"How much do we owe you?" Sam asked Jake.

Jake was like a human calculator. "Let's see. I bought all the balls they had at Budget Mart for two dollars and fifty cents. They had about forty. The others came from Price Busters. They were three dollars and twenty-five cents. So that'll be about forty-seven dollars each."

Sam tried to whistle, but his lips were too dry. "This is going to cost more than I thought."

"Yeah, I know," Jake said. "Between this and prom, my savings account will be wiped out."

"It'll be worth it," Paul assured them. "We'll still be talking about this at our twenty-five-year class reunion."

Sam couldn't imagine coming back to Bedford for the alumni banquet in twenty-five years. He'd helped the church youth group serve beverages at the banquet last year, and he just couldn't see himself as one of the guests. Then again, twenty-five years was a long time. It seemed like he'd waited forever just to reach eighteen so he could finally graduate from high school.

"We'd better wrap things up here. My grandparents are going to expect me home soon."

"Where do they think you are?" Jake asked.

"At work," Sam replied, "but I called in sick. I told Mr. Haffner I'd make up the hours later this week."

Sam looked over at the pile of colorful balls in the corner. It was going to be pretty cool seeing them rain down onto the stage on graduation day.

"Done," Jake announced, tossing his last ball into the pile.

"Why don't you go check the school one more time?" Paul suggested. "Just to make sure everybody left."

"Okay," Jake said. "I'll be right back."

Sam and Paul gathered up the beach balls and started bringing them out onto the stage.

Jake returned during their final trip. "All clear."

"Hey, good timing," Paul said. "We're ready to put these up in the net. Did you check the restrooms?"

"Yep," Jake affirmed, "and the cafeteria and the office and the hallways. The lights are off in the classrooms, and it's completely silent. It's kind of eerie, actually."

Sam set the balls in his arms onto the stage where they rolled across the wood floor. "We need a ladder."

"It should be in one of these storage areas," Jake said, lifting himself onto the stage and heading toward the back. He stepped around a bunch of metal folding chairs stacked against the wall to reach the first storage-room door. "Bingo."

Sam and Paul joined him while Jake pulled a wooden ladder out of the storage closet.

"This looks like it will be tall enough," Jake said, standing the ladder up. "Now who wants to do the honors?"

"Let Sam stand on the ladder," Paul suggested. "After all, it was his idea."

Sam walked over to the ladder and positioned it on one side of the stage. Then he climbed up the rungs until he reached the suspended vinyl netting.

"Okay," he called out to his friends. "Start tossing the balls to me."

The first ball ricocheted off the top of the ladder and the next one bounced off Sam's head.

"Hold it," Sam said. "We're never going to get anything accomplished like this. One of you stand at the base of the ladder and hand the balls up to me. The other one pick up the balls around the stage."

Paul walked over to the ladder. "You can gather up the balls, Jake, since you're so talented with them."

"Gee, thanks," Jake said as he started gathering up the balls one by one and tossing them to Paul, who then handed them up to Sam.

Sam placed them in the netting, pleased to see that the bright colors didn't show through the black vinyl fabric. And they were so lightweight no one would be able to tell there was anything up there.

It was the perfect plan.

"Is that it?" Paul called out to Jake, who was roaming around the stage.

"Hold on," Jake replied. "I think one more rolled back here."

Sam watched Jake head toward the same storage closet where he had found the ladder.

"Here it is," Jake said, leaning down to pick it up. His hip bumped against the stacked folding chairs, and they fell to the floor like dominoes.

The loud sound of the crash made Sam wince. "Way to go, Perkins."

"It was an accident," Jake said as he started to pick up the chairs.

"Toss me the ball," Paul told him. "Then we can both help you pick them up and get out of here."

Jake picked up the ball again and tossed it to Paul, who handed it to Sam.

"Mission accomplished," Sam said as he placed the last beach ball in the netting.

At that moment the auditorium door opened, and the lights flipped on. Sam's stomach dropped to his toes as he looked toward the doorway to see Dana standing there.

Fifteen minutes later, Sam was waiting outside the assistant principal's office with Paul. Dana had called Jake inside the office first.

"So much for our senior prank," Paul said mournfully. "Now we'll probably be lucky to go through the graduation ceremony at all. Well, me and Jake anyway. You'll probably get a pass since Mrs. Stevenson's your aunt."

Sam wasn't so sure. He'd seen the way Dana had looked at him. Not only would he be in trouble at school, but his grandparents were sure to find out too.

The inner office door opened, and Jake emerged with Dana right behind him.

"I'll see you tomorrow, Jake," she told him.

"Okay," Jake said, not making eye contact with the other two. That was a bad sign, in Sam's opinion.

Dana turned to the boys. "Paul, I'll see you now."

Paul glanced over at Sam and then headed for the inner office. Dana waited for him to walk inside and then closed the door behind her.

Sam sat alone in the outer office, growing more nervous by the minute. He didn't like the expression of disappointment he kept seeing on Dana's face. Leaning back against the chair, Sam closed his eyes, wondering why they'd ever come up with the stupid idea to pull a senior prank. They were so close to graduating—and now this.

Several minutes later, the door to the inner office opened, and Paul came out. He rolled his eyes as he walked by Sam and headed out the door.

"Sam?" Aunt Dana said, motioning him inside the assistant principal's office.

Sam got up, his feet feeling heavy as he followed her inside. He just wanted to go home and forget this had ever happened.

Dana rounded her desk and then waited for Sam to take a seat in the chair across from her. "Well, Sam, what do you have to say for yourself?"

He hated that question, especially when they both already knew the answer. "I messed up."

"That's for sure." Dana sighed as she folded her hands on top of the desk. "Students are not allowed to be in the school without supervision. What if you had fallen off the ladder and gotten hurt?"

"That didn't happen." Then he asked her a question. "How did you know we were there?"

"Your uncle is working late again tonight so I decided to come to school to catch up on some paperwork. I'd just walked through the front door when I heard a loud crash. It about scared me to death."

Sam swallowed a sigh, realizing they might have gotten away with it if Jake hadn't knocked over those folding chairs. He could be home eating supper right now instead of waiting for Dana to hand down his punishment.

"How much trouble are we in?" Sam asked.

"A lot," she said without hesitation. "You, Paul, and Jake will have to be at school serving detention every day until the seniors are let out."

"But I have to work after school," Sam said.

"You'll have to work that out with your boss," she said firmly. "This was a serious infraction, Sam. There has to be a serious consequence."

Sam slumped back in his chair, so frustrated and angry that he knew better than to say a word. He couldn't believe they were being punished like this because of a bunch of stupid beach balls.

"Now, do you want to tell your grandparents or should I?" Dana asked.

"I'll do it," Sam muttered. "May I go now?"

"Yes, you may," she said, not looking the least sympathetic.

Sam walked out of the office and left the school, still fuming about his punishment. A lot of good it did him to have an aunt as the assistant principal. She was even stricter than Mrs. Wellington had been.

Sam got in his car and switched on the engine. He gunned it a few times, hoping Aunt Dana could hear him. Sam shifted the car into reverse and peeled out of the parking lot, taking his anger out on the car. He didn't hate Aunt Dana, but he didn't like her much at the moment either.

THAT EVENING, Charlotte removed the boiling pot of cauliflower from the stovetop and carried it to the sink to pour it into the strainer. She'd found a recipe for mashed cauliflower that tasted surprisingly like mashed potatoes but with fewer calories. She was serving it with roast turkey breast and low-calorie gravy, a meal that was already making her mouth water.

After she drained the water, she placed the cauliflower back in the pot and turned on her hand mixer. It took only a few minutes before it looked just like mashed potatoes.

When she turned off the mixer, she heard the rumble of an engine outside. "It sounds like Sam is finally home."

Emily placed the last plate on the table and then walked over to the kitchen window and parted the curtain. "Yeah, it's Sam. It looks like Uncle Pete is pulling into the yard with the tractor too."

"Will you call the rest of the family for supper, please?"

"Okay," Emily replied heading out of the kitchen.

Charlotte liked having the old Emily back and thanked God that the battle between them seemed to be over. Emily hadn't said a word about the prom since Friday night, and she seemed resigned to the fact that she wasn't going.

Bob walked into the kitchen. "Emily said it was time to eat."

"We'll start as soon as Sam comes in," she told him. "Would you like a cup of coffee?"

"Nope," he said. "I've already had too much today. I'll be lucky if I can sleep tonight."

Bob had attended a meeting at the fire hall this morning to discuss the war reenactment. Afterward he'd gone out to Paul Hubbard's land in the afternoon to mark out where they'd be putting up the tents.

Emily and Christopher entered the kitchen and took their seats at the table as Sam walked inside the house.

"There's something I need to tell you," Sam said bluntly.

Charlotte's heart sank at his tone. This wouldn't be good.

"Me and Paul and Jake got in trouble at school," Sam continued.

"What kind of trouble?" Bob asked.

"We wanted to pull a prank for graduation so we put a bunch of beach balls in the netting above the stage in the auditorium. We were going to let them loose at the end of the ceremony."

"Oh, Sam," Charlotte chided, disappointed to hear that he was part of such a childish prank. "What were you thinking?"

Sam shrugged. "I don't know. I guess we thought it would be funny."

"I bet you're in a ton of trouble," Emily said.

"Oh, we're in trouble, all right," Sam told her. "Aunt Dana caught us, and we have to serve detention every day until the seniors' last day of classes."

Charlotte could hear the anger in his words and hated the fact that Dana had been the one to find them. She couldn't blame her daughter-in-law for Sam's punishment, but she didn't want it to cause a rift between them. It seemed like the Stevenson family was facing one skirmish after another this month.

"I thought you had to work after school today," Bob said.

Sam's gaze fell to the floor. "I called in sick."

Bob folded his arms across his chest. "So you lied to Mr. Haffner and to us?"

"Yeah," Sam said, still not able to meet Bob's gaze. "And I'll probably lose my job when I tell Mr. Haffner I won't be able to work for the next week."

Charlotte watched her grandson. He might look like a man, but he still had a lot of growing up to do. It seemed too soon to let him go out in the world on his own, but time didn't stand still. At least he'd be going to school in Grand Island instead of someplace far away from Heather Creek.

"Sit down at the table and eat," Bob said gruffly. "We'll talk about your punishment at home after we're done with supper."

Sam shuffled over to the table and sat down just as the telephone rang.

"Can you get that, Emily?" Charlotte asked her, adding the finishing touches to the mashed cauliflower.

Emily answered the phone while Christopher told Bob about his school day. A few moments later, Emily hung up the phone and turned to Bob. "Grandpa, that was Mrs. Freeman. She said one of our cows is out."

Bob started to stand up and then sat down again. "Go tell Pete," he directed Emily, "so he can take care of it."

"Aren't you going to help him?" Charlotte asked, knowing how difficult it was for just one person to round up a loose cow.

"I will if he asks me," Bob said, turning back to Christopher.

Her heart sank at his words. After their dinner at Mel's Place Charlotte had let herself believe that the feud between Bob and Pete was over. She waited while Emily went outside to relay the message to Pete, hoping her son would come in and tell Bob he needed him.

But a few moments later, Emily walked back inside. "Okay, I told him. He's on his way to take care of it."

Charlotte placed the sliced roasted turkey breast on the table, but the savory aroma didn't tempt her. She didn't feel hungry anymore. As she lowered her head for the dinner prayer, Charlotte added a silent prayer of her own. *Please, Lord, heal this family. Help us find our way back together again.*

Chapter Fourteen

"Christopher, will you come here, please?"
Christopher sat at his desk and thought about pretending that he hadn't heard Miss Luka. He'd been dreading this moment since he'd arrived at school this morning. He'd even given away half his lunch, feeling too nervous to eat much.

"Christopher?" Miss Luka prompted.

Dylan leaned toward him and whispered, "Good luck."

Christopher rose slowly from his desk and walked to Miss Luka's desk. He knew exactly what she was going to ask him but hadn't quite figured out how to answer. Now he had about five seconds left to think of something.

"Christopher," Miss Luka began, keeping her voice soft so the other students wouldn't hear her, "why haven't you turned in your interview questions yet? They have to be approved by Principal Harding by the end of the day."

"I don't know," Christopher mumbled.

Miss Luka stared at him for a long moment. "This isn't like you. Do you need help? Are you having trouble thinking of questions?"

Christopher shrugged but didn't say anything. What could he say? He had no intention of doing the interview.

That would probably get him into as much trouble as Sam, maybe more. Grandpa had punished Sam by giving him extra chores for two weekends and making him go apologize to Mr. Haffner for lying. That was on top of his school punishment.

"Is there another reason why you haven't turned in your interview questions?" Miss Luka asked. "A reason you're not telling me?"

This was his chance. Miss Luka had always been nice to him. Maybe she could get him out of this jam.

"I just don't feel like interviewing someone I don't know," he said. "I want someone else in the class to do it."

"I'm sorry, Christopher, but all the other students have already been given a project for Memorial Day. I selected you to write the article for the school newspaper because I thought you would do the best job."

Christopher looked down at the floor. He hated disappointing Miss Luka, but she just didn't understand. George Kimball wouldn't give him an interview when he saw Christopher at his door. He was probably still angry about his ruined rosebush.

Closing his eyes, he could see the elderly man shaking his cane and shouting at them as they ran away. Just thinking about coming face to face with him made Christopher's knees feel wobbly.

"You're representing the sixth-grade class," Miss Luka continued. "We're counting on you to do a good job."

He frantically searched for something to say, anything that would save him from interviewing George Kimball. He probably wouldn't even want to be interviewed. Old Man Kimball hadn't sounded nice the one time Christopher had seen him, certainly not as nice as Great-Grandpa Les had sounded in his letters.

Then it hit him.

He looked up at Miss Luka, eager to tell her his new idea. "Can I write a story about my great-grandpa instead? We have a bunch of letters he wrote when he was a soldier during World War II. They're really interesting."

"I'm sure they are," Miss Luka replied, "and I'd love to have you bring them to school and share them with the class. But you still need to write a story about Mr. Kimball. The school has already contacted him about doing the interview, and he's expecting a student to stop by next week."

Christopher's hopes faded as she spoke. He couldn't give the interview to another student, and he couldn't write a story about his great-grandpa. That meant he was in trouble. Big trouble.

"I'd like your interview questions by the end of the day," Miss Luka told him. "You can type them on the computer while the other students are working on their art projects. Just raise your hand if you get stuck."

"Okay." Christopher had no intention of interviewing Old Man Kimball, but he could delay his punishment by turning in the interview questions. Then at least he'd have another week of freedom before Miss Luka sent him to Principal Harding for his punishment.

Maybe he'd get detention like Sam and have to stay at school even after the other kids got let out for the summer. The thought made him sick, but not as sick as the prospect of facing Old Man Kimball.

When he returned to his desk, Dylan looked over at him. "Well?"

"I couldn't get out of it," Christopher said.

"Uh-oh," Dylan replied. "Now what are you going to do?"

"Nothing. They can't force me to do the interview. I'd rather get in trouble with Miss Luka and the principal than with Old Man Kimball."

"Me too," Dylan agreed. "I went over by his house the other day to spy, and he was cutting some of the burned stems off his rosebush. He didn't look too happy."

Christopher admired Dylan's bravery. He wouldn't go within a mile of Old Man Kimball. "He didn't see you, did he?"

"No, I hid really well. I could hear him muttering something though."

Now Christopher knew he'd made the right decision about the interview. If Old Man Kimball was still mad about a stupid rosebush a week after they'd shot the firecracker rocket, then he was probably crazy.

"All right, class," Miss Luka announced, rising from her desk. "We're going to work on our watercolors now. Get your art smocks out of the cupboards. The clean paintbrushes are by the sink."

Christopher wished he could go with the rest of his classmates as he watched them leave their desks. He liked to paint even though he wasn't very good at it.

Miss Luka walked over to his desk. "You can start working on your interview questions at the computer now, Christopher. If you work hard you should have some time left over to paint."

"Okay." Christopher turned and headed to the computer station.

He sat down at the computer and opened a text document.

Principal Harding had instructed the writers to come up with ten questions to ask the veterans about their service. Christopher typed a list of numbers from one to ten and tried to think of what to ask.

He knew it didn't really matter since he was never going to interview Old Man Kimball, but he had to write good questions or Miss Luka would make him redo the assignment.

Christopher placed his fingers on the keyboard and typed the question uppermost in his mind: *Have you ever thought about going back to France?*

EMILY SAT IN THE BLEACHERS of Bedford Stadium watching Troy race around the track. He was running the 1,600 meters and was near the middle of the field of runners halfway through the race.

"Go, Troy!" she shouted as the runners sprinted past the bleachers toward the finish line. She watched him shoot past the boy in front of him to come in third.

"Yay!" she cheered with the rest of the crowd. There were six teams at Bedford's invitational track meet, and Emily knew Troy was hoping to make it to state this year.

Emily left the bleachers and walked toward the small canopy the Bedford track team had set up to provide shade from the sun. Troy was standing there mopping his head with a towel, the third-place medal around his neck.

"You did great!" she said, moving in to give him a hug. "I'm so proud of you."

"I'm all sweaty," he warned, but she hugged him anyway.

"When's your next race?"

"In about half an hour," he said. "I'll need that much time to rest if I want to place in the 3,200 meters. The competition is fierce."

"Do you want me to leave?" she asked, noticing other track athletes stretched out under the canopy with earbuds in their ears.

"No, let's walk." Troy bent down to touch his toes. "I need to let my muscles cool down. If I stop moving too soon they'll tighten up."

Emily waited until they were alone to ask him the question that had been bothering her for the last two days.

"So why haven't you told me about Dean's party?"

He glanced at her and then looked away. "Where did you hear about it?"

"From Nicole. She said you're going to be there. I wish you would have told me first."

"And I wish you'd tell me if we're going to the prom or not." Troy knelt down to tie his shoe. "I haven't put down a deposit on a tux yet, but I can't wait much longer."

"I thought you were going to the prom even if I didn't go."

"I changed my mind," Troy replied. "It wouldn't be any fun without you. Besides, I could tell it was making you feel bad, and I don't care that much about it anyway. The prom is more for girls than for guys."

Emily appreciated the fact that he didn't want to go to the prom without her. "The prom is out. I tried everything, but my grandma just refuses to change her mind. It's too late now anyway, the prom is only four days away."

"There's always next year."

"I guess so," Emily said without much enthusiasm.

"Do you want to get something to eat?" Troy asked, looking over at the concession stand.

"No, I'm not hungry. Are you?"

He shook his head. "I can't eat before a race."

"So are you going to Dean's party or not?"

Troy blinked, obviously startled by the sudden change in subject. "Yeah. I told him I'd stop in for a few minutes."

"And you weren't going to tell me?"

He shrugged. "I didn't want you to feel bad. I figured if your grandparents weren't letting you go to the prom, they'd never let you go to Dean's party."

Emily walked in silence beside him, knowing he had a point. Still, she didn't like the fact that Troy was keeping secrets from her. If he wasn't going to tell her about the party, maybe he wouldn't tell her what happened *at* the party either. She trusted her boyfriend, but she didn't trust some of the girls she knew would be at Dean's party, especially Nicole Evans. It would be just like her to try and steal Troy, even if she had a prom date of her own.

"Are you mad?" Troy asked at last.

"No." A cheer erupted from the stands as another race ended. "But I want you to pick me up on your way to Dean's party."

He stared at her. "Seriously?"

She nodded. "I'm going to sneak out of the house about midnight. Everybody should be asleep by then."

"Emily," he said, shaking his head in dismay, "are you sure you want to do that?"

"Yes," she said firmly. "My grandparents will never know. You can pick me up at the bottom of the hill at midnight."

Troy hesitated. "I feel like your grandparents are just starting to like me. If they find out that I helped you sneak out . . ."

"They won't find out," Emily interjected. "I have it all planned out, right down to the last detail. Nothing can go wrong."

"Famous last words," Troy muttered, looking distinctly unhappy about his part in her plan.

"Are you going to pick me up or not?"

"What if I don't?"

"Then I'll walk there," she said, meaning every word. Emily was tired of her grandparents treating her like a child, and she was especially tired of Nicole making fun of her.

"Then I guess I don't have any choice," Troy said, heading back to the Bedford tent. "But if you change your mind on Saturday, then turn on the light in your bedroom. If I see it, I'll know not to wait for you."

"I won't change my mind," she vowed.

Chapter Fifteen

On Thursday afternoon, Christopher was out in the barn giving his lamb a lecture.

"You have to be good," Christopher said as he placed the halter on Magic.

If Magic got away . . . Christopher didn't want to think about that possibility, remembering the other times the lamb had escaped through the fence and they'd chased him all over the farm to catch him.

The lamb stood without moving, still chewing on the wad of alfalfa Christopher had offered him before reaching for the halter. If Magic behaved on this walk, Christopher planned to take him on longer and longer walks to prepare him for the Memorial Day celebration.

"Okay, let's go," Christopher told him, leading the lamb out the barn door.

He saw Pete over by the fuel tanks filling the tractor and headed in that direction.

"Well, look at that," Pete exclaimed when he saw them coming. "Looks like you've tamed Magic."

"We're going for a walk around the farm to practice for the petting zoo in the park."

"That sounds like a good idea," Pete said as he checked the oil. "Mom told me that Jim Dickerson is coming out to shear him this afternoon."

"Yeah. I think Magic's a little nervous about it."

"There's nothing to be nervous about," Pete said, wiping his oily hands on his jeans. "It won't hurt him, and he'll love having all that heavy wool off of him now that it's getting warmer."

"That's what Grandma said." Christopher reached out to pet the lamb. "But he won't look the same. I wonder how long it will take to grow back."

"Not as long as you'd think," Pete replied. "He'll probably look just the way he does now by the time the county fair rolls around."

"Good," Christopher said, worried that the shear job would make Magic look silly. Sometimes the other kids at school would tease him when he got a haircut. He didn't want the same thing to happen to Magic.

"Where's your brother?"

"He's serving detention at school," Christopher replied. "Aunt Dana's the one who caught him."

"Oh, that's right," Pete said. "She told me about that." Then he grinned. "It did sound like a pretty good prank, but don't tell her I said that."

"I won't," Christopher promised. "Sam almost got fired when he told Mr. Haffner he'd lied to him, but Mr. Haffner's giving him one more chance. He's got to work after detention today so he won't get to see Magic get sheared."

"I wish I could stick around and watch," Pete said, "but I need to get back to the field."

"Will you be done planting in time to do the war reenactment with us?" Christopher asked.

Pete didn't say anything, keeping his gaze on the herbicide sprayer. "Not this year. I'm just too busy with the farm."

"Grandpa could help you." Christopher knew that his grandpa wasn't working on the farm lately, but he wasn't sure why. Sam had told him that Pete and Grandpa had gotten into an argument, but they seemed to be getting along now. When Christopher had arrived home from school today Uncle Pete had been sitting at the kitchen table talking to Grandpa about the College World Series in Omaha.

"I'm going to head out now," Pete said, walking toward the door of the tractor. "Dana will be bringing my supper out later. If I'm not back yet, just send her to the south forty on Sawchuck's Quarter."

"Okay," Christopher said, leading Magic quickly away from the tractor. He didn't want the loud noise of the engine to startle his lamb.

He walked toward the front yard and rounded the house, surprised to see his grandpa up on a ladder. He held a hammer in one hand and nails in the other.

"What are you doing, Grandpa?"

"Fixing some loose siding," Grandpa said. He stood on the ladder near Sam's bedroom window. "Your grandma had me fix a piece of siding the other day, and I just keep finding more loose pieces."

"I'm taking Magic for a walk," Christopher told him.

"Okay," Grandpa replied, placing a nail against a piece of siding. "Stay out of trouble."

At the first loud crack of the hammer against the siding,

Magic jumped and shot forward. Christopher barely held on to the halter as the lamb pulled him around the other side of the house.

"Magic, stop!" Christopher shouted.

But Magic didn't listen and raced toward the backyard while Christopher ran behind him trying to keep up. He saw Emily near her garden and yelled for help.

"Emily!"

She looked up and started laughing; then she rose to her feet and hurried over to grab Magic.

"Whoa there," she said gently, holding him firmly.

The lamb tried to buck against her once, but Emily didn't let go.

Christopher was gasping for breath as he moved his hands down the halter's lead rope until they were only inches away from Magic's head. "I've got him now."

"Are you sure?" Emily said, still clutching handfuls of wool.

"Yeah, I'm sure."

Emily grinned. "Looks like Magic still needs some practice with the halter."

"That's why I brought him out here," Christopher replied. "He was doing great until Grandpa started hammering, and the noise scared him."

"There will be noise at the park too. You'd better not let him pull you around there."

Christopher looked down at his lamb. "Do you hear that, Magic? You can't mess up in the park, so you'd better get it all out of your system now."

Emily headed back toward her garden. Then she turned

and motioned to Christopher. "Can you help me for a minute?"

He followed her, Magic now walking docilely by his side. Christopher could see rolls of chicken wire on the ground next to her garden. "What do you want?"

Emily picked up a length of chicken wire. "The rabbits have started nibbling at some of my plants, so I need to put this around my garden. I want you to hold up this end while I tie the other end to the post."

"Okay, give me a minute." Christopher tied Magic's lead rope around the stump of a bush, giving it a quick tug to make sure it was secure before going over to help Emily.

He saw four pieces of rebar sticking out of the ground, one in each corner of her garden. The vegetables were planted in rows, and at the end of each row was a Popsicle stick with the name of the vegetable on it. At the back of the garden was a big patch of strawberry plants.

"Hold this," Emily directed him, placing one end of the chicken wire in his hands.

Christopher watched as she bent down and started attaching the chicken wire to the rebar. It barely reached his knees. "Will this be high enough to keep the rabbits out?"

"Grandma told me it would be, and she's been planting gardens for years and years."

Christopher watched his sister work, his mouth already watering in anticipation of the strawberries she'd planted. He liked carrots and radishes too but wasn't as crazy about tomatoes and green peppers.

"What is bok choy?" he asked her, reading one of the Popsicle sticks.

"It's a Chinese vegetable," Emily replied, "kind of like cabbage."

She took the other end of the chicken wire from Christopher and knelt down to attach it to another rebar post. "Mom used to make it all the time, remember?"

"No," Christopher said, glancing over at Magic. The lamb looked perfectly happy snacking on the green grass. "Did I like it?"

"I think so." Emily rose to her feet. "There. One side is done. Now help me with the next side."

Christopher followed her around the edge of the garden holding up the chicken wire while she attached it to the post. It bothered him that he didn't remember eating bok choy. There were a lot of things he didn't remember about his life in California. It seemed the older he got, the more those memories faded away.

"Do you think he'll come to Sam's graduation?" Christopher asked his sister.

Emily studied him for a moment until she realized what he was saying. "You mean Dad?"

Christopher nodded. They hadn't talked about their father much lately, but they both knew that Sam had invited him. Christopher hadn't seen his dad since Christmas, although he had e-mailed him a few times.

"I don't know," Emily said, turning back to her work. "Maybe, but I wouldn't count on it."

Christopher was about to ask Emily if she wanted to see him again when a noise in the driveway caught his attention. He looked over to see a black pickup truck pull up next to the barn.

"That must be Mr. Dickerson," he said. Then he noticed someone in the passenger seat as well.

"Who's Mr. Dickerson?"

"The man who's going to shear Magic."

Then the passenger door opened, and Christopher saw a cane slowly lower to the ground. Dread filled him when an elderly man slowly climbed out of the truck.

It was Old Man Kimball.

Chapter Sixteen

Charlotte was sweeping the mud porch when she looked out the window and saw Jim Dickerson and his uncle, George Kimball, walking toward the barn. She set her broom aside and hurried outside to greet them.

"Hello there," Charlotte said when she reached the barn.

"Hello, Charlotte." Jim glanced toward the house. "Looks like you folks are busy today. I see Bob's up on a ladder."

"He's doing some repairs," she said and then turned to George. "How are you, George? I haven't seen you for a while."

"I've been keeping busy." George smiled. "Of course, at my age, just getting out of bed in the morning takes up half the day."

The ninety-eight-year-old actually moved pretty well. George's wife, Helen, had been Charlotte's Sunday-school teacher when she was a child. Helen had passed away two years ago, leaving George alone in their big house on Locust Street. She was surprised he hadn't moved into a smaller place with less upkeep, but she couldn't really blame him for not wanting to leave the home he'd lived in for more than fifty years.

"Do you have time to come in for a cup of coffee?" she asked the men.

"I'm afraid not," Jim told her. "We've got a few more stops to make today."

"Then we'd better get to it." She looked around but didn't see Christopher or Magic in the corral. "Christopher?" she called out, wondering if he was inside the barn. "Mr. Dickerson's here to shear Magic."

When there was no response, she walked inside the barn, but there was no sign of her grandson or the lamb. "That's strange," she told the men when she walked back outside. "They've got to be around here somewhere. I told Christopher you were coming today."

George squinted as he looked down at the dirt. "Looks like there's some fresh hoof prints here. Maybe the lamb got out."

"Oh, I hope not," Charlotte exclaimed. "Magic's hard to chase down."

Charlotte's gaze scanned the yard. She could see Emily working on her garden and heard Bob nailing siding onto the house, but there was no sign of Christopher.

"No big hurry," Jim said, moving toward his truck. "I should probably sharpen the blades on my shears anyway."

Charlotte walked over to the house and found Bob just coming down off the ladder. "Have you seen Christopher?"

"He and Magic walked by here a little while ago."

"Well, Jim is here to shear Magic, and now I can't find either of them. Where could he be?"

"I don't know." Bob set down the hammer and nails. "But I can help you look."

"Why don't you check by the grain bins," Charlotte suggested. "Maybe he wanted to let Magic eat some of the grain that spilled there. I'll ask Emily if she's seen him."

"Okay," Bob said, heading toward the grain bins.

The high-pitched squeal of a blade sharpener cut through the air. Charlotte thought Christopher would surely hear it and realize that Jim had arrived. But as she walked toward Emily's garden she didn't see any sign of her grandson or his lamb.

"How do you like my fence, Grandma?" Emily asked as Charlotte approached her. "Do you think it will keep the rabbits out?"

"It looks good to me," Charlotte told her. "Have you seen your brother? Jim Dickerson is here to shear Magic."

Emily smiled. "So that explains it. Christopher untied Magic from that bush and took off when he saw the black truck park by the barn."

"Took off to where?"

Emily hitched her thumb over her shoulder. "Back toward the windbreak."

Charlotte shook her head in confusion. "Now why would he do that?"

"I don't know. He seemed perfectly fine before the truck arrived . . ." Emily hesitated a moment and then met Charlotte's gaze. "Except that he was asking me about Dad."

The words turned Charlotte's frustration into concern. "What about him?"

"He wanted to know if I thought Dad would come to Sam's graduation."

Charlotte didn't say anything, wondering if Christopher wanted him to come. Kevin had shown up out of the blue at Christmas and turned all of their lives upside down before he took off again. She knew Christopher had e-mailed Kevin a few times for a class project, but he hadn't talked about him for quite a while now.

"Do you know why he brought him up?"

Emily shrugged. "Not really. We were talking about bok choy, and I told him Mom used to make it a lot when we lived in California. It seemed to bother Christopher that he couldn't remember eating it before."

Charlotte sighed. It didn't really make sense, but despite having two sons of her own she wasn't really an expert in navigating the mind of a twelve-year-old boy. "I suppose I'd better go find him."

She met Bob on the way to the windbreak.

"He's not by the grain bins," Bob told her.

"Emily said he took off toward the windbreak as soon as he saw Jim arrive."

Bob scowled. "Now why would he do that?"

Charlotte didn't say anything, not wanting to bring up the subject of Kevin Slater. Bob had disagreed with inviting Kevin to Sam's graduation even when Charlotte told him that Sam had requested it.

When they reached the windbreak, Charlotte called for him. "Christopher, please come out here. Jim is waiting, and he has a busy schedule today."

She heard the rustle of grass but knew it could simply be a rabbit or pheasant startled by the sound of her voice. "Please, Christopher," she called again. "Come out now."

When her plea didn't work, Bob took a harsher approach. "Christopher Slater," he thundered, "you'd better come out of there by the time I count to three. One, two . . ."

Charlotte heard a rustle of branches a few feet away, and then Christopher emerged with Magic from a lush thicket of trees. "Here I am."

"What do you think you're doing back here?" Bob asked him. "Mr. Dickerson is waiting to shear Magic. Now get back to the barn."

Christopher chewed his lower lip as he held out the lead rope. "Will you take him?"

"Christopher," Charlotte said in surprise, "there's no need to be afraid. I've told you that shearing doesn't hurt a lamb at all."

Christopher stared down at the ground. "I just don't want to go."

Bob took a step toward him. "Magic is your 4-H project, so you need to take responsibility for him. I want you to take your lamb to the barn. *Now.*"

Christopher looked up at his grandfather and visibly swallowed. "Okay, but will you come with me?"

Their grandson looked absolutely terrified. Charlotte didn't understand his reaction and sensed something more was going on here. But Jim was waiting for them, so the reason would have to wait.

"Yes," she told Christopher, "we'll go with you."

He took a deep breath as he turned toward the barn, acting as if he were headed toward an execution. "Okay, Magic, I guess we have to go."

As they got closer to the barn, Christopher moved slower

and slower. Charlotte could see Jim and George standing at the back of the pickup waiting for them.

"This must be Christopher," Jim said.

"Christopher, this is Mr. Dickerson," Charlotte told him, making the introductions, "and Mr. Kimball."

"You can call me Uncle George if you want," George said, smiling down at Christopher. "That's what most of the kids in my neighborhood call me."

Christopher slowly looked up at George. "They do?"

George nodded. "The ones that come around. I have the candy jar ready for any child who knocks on my door."

Charlotte smiled when she saw Christopher visibly relax. Whatever had been bothering him seemed to have evaporated when George started talking. She looked over at Bob, who looked just as puzzled by their grandson's behavior.

"And this must be Magic," Jim said, grabbing his clippers and walking toward the lamb. He looked over at Christopher. "Would you plug in the cord for me?"

"Sure," Christopher said, leaning down to grab the end of the long, orange extension cord and carrying it into the barn. A moment later, he called out. "Okay, it's plugged in."

Jim gently grabbed Magic and sat him on his hindquarters before flipping on the clippers. To Charlotte's amazement, the lamb was half sheared by the time Christopher reemerged from the barn.

"Cool!" Christopher exclaimed.

Charlotte agreed, watching the strips of wool peel off Magic's body as the shears moved over him. George slowly gathered the wool, using his cane to move it into a pile, and then placed the wool into a canvas bag.

Less than five minutes later, Jim released Magic, and the lamb shook himself as he got on all four legs again.

Christopher stared at his lamb. "He looks naked."

Charlotte laughed. "Skinny too. Poor Magic looks only half as big now that he's lost his thick coat of wool."

"I wish it was that easy for me," Bob quipped.

"Don't we all," Jim agreed, patting his big stomach.

"How much do we owe you?" Bob said, reaching for his wallet.

Jim waved him off. "You probably won't owe me anything after I sell the wool. If you do, I'll send you a bill."

Charlotte placed her hand on Christopher's shoulders. "What do you tell Mr. Dickerson?"

"Thank you for shearing Magic. It didn't seem to bother him at all, even if he does look kind of silly."

Jim smiled as he placed his clippers in the back of his truck. "Don't worry. He'll start looking better in a day or two." Then he looked at his uncle. "We'd better get going, Uncle George. We've got more sheep waiting for us."

George Kimball extended a gnarled hand to Christopher. "It was nice meeting you, young man."

Christopher reached out to shake his hand. "Nice to meet you too."

CHARLOTTE AND CHRISTOPHER WAVED as Jim's pickup turned onto Heather Creek Road.

"He wasn't as scary as I thought," Christopher said as Magic nibbled on his back pocket.

"Who? Mr. Dickerson?"

"No, Mr. Kimball."

She turned to look at him, puzzled by the comment. "Why would you think Mr. Kimball would be scary? We didn't even know he was coming today."

Christopher's cheeks turned pink. "I don't know. I just did."

Her intuition kicked in. "Is there something you're not telling me?"

Christopher kicked at a small pebble on the gravel drive. "Well, Dylan lives by Mr. Kimball, and he thinks he's scary."

"Has Dylan ever met him?"

Christopher hesitated. "No, but he's seen him in his yard before. One time Mr. Kimball even shook his cane at him."

"Well, that doesn't sound like the George Kimball I know." She gently nudged the lamb away from Christopher's back pocket. "He loves children. Maybe Dylan should stop by his house and introduce himself."

"I'll tell him," Christopher said. "I think he'll be really surprised."

Charlotte still felt there was something Christopher wasn't telling her, but before she could ask him, Dana's car pulled into the driveway.

"Pete must be working late again tonight," Charlotte said as she and Christopher walked over to greet her.

"Hello," Dana said, climbing out of the car with a picnic basket in her hands. Then she did a double take when she saw the lamb. "Is that Magic?"

Charlotte smiled. "He looks different, doesn't he? Jim Dickerson was just out here."

Dana nodded. "I heard some of the kids at school talking about getting their 4-H lambs sheared today." She looked at Christopher. "How did Magic like having all his wool shaved off?"

"I think he liked it okay," Christopher said, reaching down to pet the lamb. "He's probably hungry now. Are you hungry, boy?"

Magic responded by trying to chew off Christopher's pocket again.

"Why don't you take him back to the barn and feed him," Charlotte suggested.

"Okay." Christopher wheeled Magic around and started toward the barn; then he looked back over his shoulder. "Oh, I almost forgot. Aunt Dana, I'm supposed to tell you that Uncle Pete is on the south forty of Sawchuck's Quarter."

"Thanks, Christopher," Dana called after him.

Charlotte sighed. "I see Pete's working late again tonight."

"Tonight and every night," Dana said. "What are we going to do with our husbands?"

"I don't know," Charlotte said honestly. "They're both too stubborn for their own good. Bob's waiting for Pete to ask him for help."

"I'm not sure that will happen. He's still upset about losing that forty acres of soybeans."

"I don't think it was all Bob's fault," Charlotte said, coming to the defense of her husband.

"Oh, I don't either. If you ask me, Pete's at least half to blame, but he won't admit it. He told me this morning that he's planting that south forty with short-season corn. Maybe once that crop's in the ground he'll be able to let it go."

"I hope so. I don't like this rift between them."

"Neither do I." Dana opened her car door and placed the picnic basket on the seat. "What's Bob been doing with his time?"

"Making small repairs around the house," Charlotte said. "Planning the war reenactment has been keeping him quite busy too. I'm afraid once that's over he'll start driving me crazy looking for something to do."

"Surely this can't go on forever," Dana said. "Pete needs his dad's help around the farm or he's going to run himself ragged. It will be a little easier when our house is done and we're living out here, but that's not going to happen for a while yet."

"I'll keep working on Bob," Charlotte told her, "if you keep working on Pete."

"I will," Dana promised, "but I'm not sure how much good it will do."

Charlotte didn't have any advice to give her. Pete had always gone his own way. "At least they're talking to each other."

"Yes, but about everything except the farm. I just don't understand it."

Charlotte didn't either, although she sensed it was part of the long separation process that happened when a son started taking over the family farm. Soon Pete would be living in his own house on Heather Creek Farm and, God willing, raising his own family. Maybe Bob was feeling that he really wasn't needed anymore. That would be a tough nut to swallow for any farmer.

"Okay, enough about our husbands," Dana said with a smile. "Are you going to the promenade Saturday night?"

Charlotte shook her head. "No, I'm skipping it this year. Emily doesn't want to go, and I promised Sam I wouldn't make a big deal out of it this year. Arielle's parents will be giving us some pictures of the two of them."

Dana's smile faded. "Sam barely said two words to me during detention today. I think he's still angry about the punishment I doled out."

"You only did what you thought was right."

"Do you think I'm being too hard on the boys? I'm still getting used to this assistant principal gig, and I'll be so glad when school is out for the summer. I'm just not good at playing the heavy."

"No, I don't think you were too hard on them," Charlotte assured. "Those three boys knew perfectly well that what they were doing was wrong. I'm just sorry that Sam put you in this position."

"I'll be glad when their detention is over and we can focus on graduation next Saturday. I still want to help decorate for Sam's party, if you think he won't mind."

"You're his aunt now; I'm sure he won't mind at all." Charlotte thought for a moment. "Let's plan on decorating next Friday evening. That way all I need to worry about on Saturday is making food for the reception."

"Okay, I'll see you Friday evening," Dana said, climbing back into her car. "Now I'd better go feed Pete his supper and try to talk some sense into him."

"Good luck," Charlotte said, knowing Dana was going to need it.

As she watched Dana drive away, Charlotte prayed that she'd be successful. "Lord, please open Pete's heart and let him see how much he and Bob need each other."

Chapter Seventeen

Emily watched the credits roll on the television screen after the Saturday night western, wondering if her grandparents would ever go to bed. It was almost eleven o'clock, and she had a lot to do before it was time to meet Troy on Heather Creek Road.

"It's time to hit the hay," Bob said, lowering the recliner.

Emily breathed a sigh of relief at his words and watched her grandma set aside her embroidery.

"It *is* getting late, isn't it," Charlotte said, checking her watch.

"Are you going to stay up until Sam gets home?" Bob asked her.

Emily held her breath, waiting for Grandma to reply.

"I don't think so," Charlotte said at last. She placed her embroidery in the basket they'd given her for Mother's Day. "He promised to be home by one o'clock, and I think he knows better than to break his word after what happened this last week."

"I hope you're right," Bob said, rising to his feet.

"I'll keep our bedroom door open," Charlotte said, "so I can hear him come in."

With that bit of information, Emily knew she'd have to be extra quiet if she wanted to sneak out of the house tonight. She'd checked the front door earlier today, just to make sure it wouldn't squeak when she opened it. Everything was going as planned so far, but she needed everyone asleep as soon as possible.

"Hey, Christopher," she said, leaning down to shake her brother's shoulder, "wake up. You need to go to bed."

Christopher's eyes fluttered open. "What?"

"It's time for bed," Emily repeated.

He blinked a few times and then slowly sat up. "Is the movie over?"

"It ended about five minutes ago," she told him. "Let's go upstairs."

"I don't want to go to bed yet," Christopher whined, looking at his grandparents. "Can I stay up and watch another movie on the DVD player? Please?"

Charlotte shook her head. "We have church tomorrow, so you need a good night's sleep."

"I already got some sleep," Christopher countered. "I'm not tired at all anymore."

"You heard your grandma," Bob said. "Get upstairs, young man."

Christopher made a face as he walked out of the family room. "Okay, I'm going."

"I'll be up in a few minutes to tuck you in," Charlotte called after him.

"Good-night," Emily said as she followed her brother. She knew her grandma might check on her when she came to tuck Christopher in, so she had to make it look like she was going to bed.

"I call the bathroom first," Emily told Christopher, scooting ahead of him on the stairs.

"That's not fair either," Christopher complained, obviously still grumpy.

"I'll hurry," she promised as they reached the top of the stairs. She slipped into the bathroom and brushed her teeth and then ran a comb through her hair. She'd used the curling iron on it earlier in the day and added enough hairspray for it to keep its shape.

Emily emerged from the bathroom and then stopped by Christopher's open door to tell him the bathroom was free. But when she looked inside she could see that he was already fast asleep on his bed. She walked inside and covered him with the blanket, grateful that he'd put on his pajamas before the movie so she didn't have to wake him up again.

Emily left his bedroom and walked to her own, closing the door behind her. Then she donned her pajamas and slipped into bed. Her heart beat a mile a minute while she waited to hear her grandmother's step on the stairs. Her gaze moved to the clock on the bed stand, and she watched the minutes tick by.

After what seemed like an eternity, Emily's door cracked open.

"Good-night, Emily," Charlotte told her.

Emily faked a yawn. "Good-night, Grandma."

The door closed again, and Emily waited until she heard Charlotte descending the stairs before she dared to get out of bed. She slid her hand under the box springs and pulled out the backpack she'd stashed there earlier. Her party clothes and shoes were inside, along with a comb and her makeup kit. She planned to get dressed in the barn once she made it outside. Then she would fix her hair and apply her makeup in Troy's truck. This way, if her grandma caught her coming down the stairs, she'd still be in her pajamas. She'd have to find a way to explain the backpack, but she'd simply say she couldn't sleep and wanted to work on homework in the kitchen.

Emily crept over to the air vent and lay down on the floor, her ear pressed against the grate. She could hear the faint voices of her grandparents but couldn't make out what they were saying. She lay there until she couldn't hear their voices anymore, only the silence of the night.

Slowly rising to her feet, Emily slipped the backpack over one shoulder and then turned to watch the clock. She figured if she left the house by ten minutes till midnight that would give her enough time to change into her clothes and walk to the bottom of Heather Creek Road to meet Troy.

When eleven fifty arrived, Emily slid her stocking-clad feet quietly across the floor until she reached the door. She opened it just far enough to stick her head out and listen for any sound from below.

When she didn't hear anything, she crept out of her room and closed the door behind her again. Emily made it down the stairs without making a sound and tiptoed across the living-room carpet to the front door.

She stood with her hand on the doorknob and waited a few moments, but all she heard was her snoring grandfather. The coast was clear.

Opening the door, Emily stepped outside and then closed it quietly behind her again. She was greeted by the chirping of crickets and the far-off howl of a coyote.

SENTIMENTAL JOURNEY | 153

"I made it," she whispered to herself, relief flowing through her.

The full moon illuminated the farmyard, and Emily wondered if Troy was at their designated spot yet. As she walked toward the barn, she thought she saw something moving out of the corner of her eye. Turning slightly, Emily looked toward her garden and saw two raccoons inside the chicken wire fence she'd just put up on Thursday.

"Oh, no," Emily muttered under her breath as she turned around and raced toward the garden. When she reached it, she tossed aside her backpack and looked for something to throw at the ravaging raccoons.

All she could find was a scoop shovel propped on a fence post near the chicken coop. She ran over to pick it up and then returned to her garden to shoo the raccoons away.

"Get out of here," she said in a low voice, swinging the shovel at them. The raccoons stared at her, their ears perked up.

She swung again, accidentally hitting the corner of the shovel on a piece of the rebar. The clang of metal on metal broke the peaceful quiet. A moment later, Toby started barking.

"Oh, no!" Emily cried as the dog raced toward her. Toby's barking intensified when she saw the raccoons. When they saw the dog, they quickly climbed over the fence, the top of the wire bending and then collapsing under their weight, and then scampered toward the windbreak. Toby chased after them, barking all the way.

Any hope Emily had that her grandparents had slept through the commotion were dashed when she saw a light appear in the kitchen window. A moment later, her grandpa emerged from the house, pulling the straps of his overalls over his shoulders. Grandma followed close behind him.

"Emily, what are you doing out here?" he demanded.

Emily knew Troy was probably waiting for her at the bottom of Heather Creek Road. She just hoped he didn't do anything crazy like drive past the house to look for her.

"I heard a noise," Emily lied, "and looked out my window. That's when I saw raccoons in my garden. So I came outside to scare them away, and Toby chased them off."

"You know better than to approach a wild animal," Bob said. "You could have gotten hurt."

"I'm sorry," Emily said, trying not to cry.

"Go back inside," Charlotte said, wrapping her terrycloth robe more tightly around her. "Grandpa and I will set your fence back up."

"Okay," Emily agreed, aware that she needed to turn on her bedroom light so Troy would know her plan had failed. He'd probably be relieved.

She just hoped Troy didn't tell anyone at the party about her plan to sneak out tonight, especially if Nicole was around to hear it.

As she headed toward the house, Emily let the tears fall. Her night was ruined. Now she'd never make it to the party.

"**PULL IT A LITTLE TIGHTER,**" Bob told Charlotte as he wrapped a piece of wire attaching the chicken wire to the rebar.

Charlotte couldn't believe she was standing outside in her robe and slippers like this. Something about Emily's story didn't make sense, but it was her attitude more than her words that made Charlotte uneasy.

"Okay, I've got it," Bob said, walking over to take the other end of the fence from her. He bent down to attach it to the rebar. "Do you see any wire around here?"

Charlotte looked around, knowing it would be hard to find with the full moon providing the only light. "No."

"It's got to be around here somewhere," Bob said, brushing one hand through the grass.

Charlotte started searching farther away from the garden, wondering if the wire had flown off when the raccoons had climbed the fence. She saw something odd at the base of a shrub. It wasn't a piece of wire though; it was something much bigger.

"Found it," Bob called, placing the wire around the rebar post.

She walked over to the shrub and picked up Emily's backpack. "This is odd."

"What?"

She walked back to the garden. "Emily's backpack was under that shrub."

Bob shook his head. "I can't believe how those kids leave things lying around. She probably came straight to her garden when she got out of school yesterday and left it out here all this time. She's lucky it didn't rain."

Charlotte wasn't convinced. She opened the backpack and found Emily's clothes and shoes inside. "I don't think she forgot anything. Look."

She pulled out a pair of jeans. "There are shoes in here too, as well as her makeup bag and hair bands."

Bob rose slowly to his feet, wincing a little as his knees cracked. "She was running away?"

"I don't think so. She didn't pack anything else." Charlotte placed the jeans back in the backpack. "It looks to me like she was sneaking out tonight."

"Now why would she do a thing like that?"

"The prom," she reminded him. "You know how much she wanted to go with Troy. I thought she'd finally accepted our decision, but I guess I was wrong."

"The prom will be over by now," Bob replied. "Besides, those aren't prom clothes."

He had a point. "Well, she was headed somewhere. I don't know if she was planning to walk there or ride Princess, but it looks like those raccoons ruined her plans."

Headlights crested the hill of Heather Creek Road, drawing their attention.

"Looks like Sam's home early," Bob said.

Charlotte followed him to the driveway as Sam pulled his Datsun 240-Z into the yard and parked it next to the house. He got out of the car, looking just as dashing in his black tuxedo as when he'd left.

"What are you two doing out here?" Sam asked.

"I'll let your grandpa tell you," Charlotte said, eager to have a word with her granddaughter. "How was the prom?"

"Okay, I guess," Sam said, loosening his tie. "The food was good."

She wanted to hear all about it, but that would have to wait until tomorrow. The more she thought about Emily's deception, the more upset she became.

It was Denise all over again.

"I'm going to take this back to Emily," Charlotte told

Bob, holding up the backpack. Then she headed toward the house. As she walked, she could hear Bob telling Sam about the raccoon attack on Emily's garden.

When she reached Emily's room, she saw the door open and the light on inside. Emily sat on the bed, tears shining on her cheeks.

Charlotte walked up to her and held out the backpack. "You left this outside."

Emily looked down at the floor. "I thought you might find it."

"Care to explain what it was doing out there?" Charlotte asked as she set the backpack on the bed. "And no more lies, please. I think I've heard enough for one night."

Emily wiped the tears off her cheeks. "I was going to Dean Wallace's party."

"Really? And how were you planning to get there?"

When Emily didn't say anything, Charlotte guessed the answer. "Troy was going to pick you up?"

"He didn't want to," Emily said in his defense. "In fact, he told me that sneaking out tonight was a really bad idea, but I told him I was going, no matter what."

It bothered Charlotte that Troy Vanderveen seemed to have better judgment than Emily. She sat down on the bed next to her, saddened by the realization that Emily had simply been putting on an act these last few days. She must have been planning this for a while now.

"I know I deserve to be punished," Emily continued, tears filling her eyes once more. "But believe me, Grandma, nothing could possibly make me feel worse than I do right now."

Charlotte did believe her, but it didn't make either of them feel better. "Do you think I like saying no to you?"

Emily looked puzzled by the question. "What do you mean?"

"I know how much you wanted to go to the prom," Charlotte said. "And I also know that you don't always understand why Grandpa and I sometimes forbid you from doing something."

Emily sniffed, temporarily stanching her tears. "No, I don't understand."

"That's because you're sixteen years old," Charlotte said gently. "Grandpa and I have been through this kind of thing before with your mom. We didn't want her to date your dad because we thought she was too young and we didn't know Kevin at all. It caused all kinds of problems between us."

Charlotte was quiet for a moment, praying that God would guide her to say the right things.

"Is that why she ran away with him?" Emily asked. "Because you were too strict?"

"It's one of the reasons." Charlotte sighed. "I still remember how I felt that day when I realized she'd run away. It was one of the worst days of my life."

Emily looked at her. "I wasn't running away, Grandma."

"I know," Charlotte told her. "But you still disobeyed me and Grandpa. We're not trying to make your life miserable, Emily. Just the opposite, in fact. Sometimes it's so tempting to let you do whatever you want. But I know that's not good for you. I also know that your mom wouldn't want me to do that."

Tears spilled onto Emily's cheeks. "I really miss her sometimes."

"Me too," Charlotte said, drawing her into her arms.

They both cried for a while, Charlotte gently patting Emily's head and praying that God could heal Emily's heart of the pain losing her mother had caused.

After several minutes, Emily pulled away from her. "I'm sorry I tried to sneak out, Grandma. If Nicole hadn't made fun of me for not going to the prom, I probably never would have done it."

"You're giving Nicole a lot of power over your life," Charlotte told her. "It sounds like she's able to make you do things you don't want to do."

Emily blinked. "I guess I did let her get to me."

"You've got to learn to ignore her," Charlotte said, repeating something she'd said numerous times before. "That's part of growing up."

"I'll try," Emily replied. "It won't be easy though."

Charlotte rose to her feet. "Why don't you get in bed now. It's getting late, and we can talk about this more tomorrow."

"Okay." Emily pulled back the covers and climbed inside. "Is my victory garden ruined?"

"The raccoons pulled out a few strawberry plants, but you still have a lot left. Now that Toby has their scent, I doubt they'll be back."

"I hope not."

Charlotte pulled the covers up over Emily and then leaned down to kiss her forehead. "Good-night. I love you."

"I know," Emily said, sounding like she meant it. "I love you too."

Chapter Eighteen

On Monday afternoon, Christopher walked along Locust Street on his way to George Kimball's house to conduct his interview. Dylan walked beside him, trying to tell him all the reasons he shouldn't go there.

"Old Man Kimball is crazy," Dylan proclaimed. "He'll probably whack you with his cane as soon as he sees you because you blew up his rosebush."

"He will not," Christopher insisted. "First of all, I didn't blow up his rosebush. There was just a little fire. And second, he seemed really nice out at the farm. I don't think he's the kind of guy who whacks kids with his cane."

Dylan shook his head. "Don't you see? He couldn't whack you in front of your grandma. That's why he invited you to come by for some candy. It's like the witch in that story."

Christopher thought for a moment, trying to place what story Dylan meant. "You mean 'Hansel and Gretel'?"

"That's right. Remember how she made a house out of candy so all the little kids would come and eat off of it? Then she ate them instead."

"That was just a story," Christopher told him. "It didn't really happen."

"I still think this is a big mistake."

The more Dylan talked, the more Christopher started to wonder if he *was* making a mistake. Uncle George had seemed nice enough on the farm, but Mr. Dickerson and Grandma wouldn't be around to protect him if Uncle George suddenly remembered that he'd seen him before.

Christopher slowed his step, thinking it over. "He just didn't seem mean."

"How can you say that?" Dylan asked. "Remember how he looked when there was smoke coming out of his rosebush? He looked plenty mean then."

Christopher remembered. He also remembered how terrified he'd been running away from him. Still, they hadn't been standing that close to Uncle George when it happened, and he was a really old man. He probably didn't see very well anymore.

"I have to do this interview," Christopher said at last. "Miss Luka is expecting the rough draft tomorrow. If I don't turn it in, I'll be in big trouble."

"It's your funeral," Dylan said, his body twitching. "Don't tell me I didn't warn you." He stopped about a block away from George Kimball's house.

"Are you coming?" Christopher asked him.

"Nope, I'm not crazy."

"That's probably a good idea," Christopher said. "Just because Uncle George didn't recognize me doesn't mean he wouldn't recognize you."

"I'll wait here for you," Dylan promised. "If you're not back in an hour, I'll call the police."

Christopher rolled his eyes. "Don't call the police. If you're really worried about me, call my grandma. She'll know what to do."

"Okay." Dylan edged behind an overgrown lilac bush. "Good luck."

Christopher squared his shoulders and marched the rest of the distance to the Kimball house. He mounted the porch steps and then knocked on the door.

Nobody answered.

Christopher raised his fist and knocked louder. If Uncle George couldn't see very well, he probably couldn't hear very well either.

After a while it seemed apparent to Christopher that nobody was home. *Maybe he went sheep-shearing with his nephew again*, Christopher thought to himself as he turned around. He bounded down the steps, feeling both disappointed and relieved.

"Christopher?"

He looked up and saw George Kimball walking toward him from the backyard. His stomach flip-flopped, but he made himself move forward to meet him.

"I see you stopped by for some of my candy." George smiled down at him. "Well, come on inside. I'll let you pick what you want from the bowl."

Christopher followed him back up the porch stairs, much slower this time since George was using a cane. Then they walked into the house.

"There it is," George said, pointing to the coffee table with his cane. "Help yourself."

Christopher walked over to the coffee table and stared down at the bowl full of assorted hard candies. "Butterscotch is my favorite."

"Mine too," George told him.

Christopher took a piece of candy and then turned around to tell him the real reason he'd come today. "I've been assigned to interview you about World War II."

George's white eyebrows rose in surprise. "Principal Harding told me they'd be sending a student over here to interview me. I had no idea it would be you. How come you didn't say anything about it when I was out at your place?"

Christopher struggled to think of a response, knowing he couldn't tell him the real reason. "I wanted it to be a surprise."

"Well, it certainly is that," George said, his blue eyes twinkling. "A very nice surprise."

Christopher pulled the interview questions out of his back pocket while George took a seat on the sofa.

"Do you have a pencil?" Christopher asked him.

"Over there on my desk," George said, pointing with his cane.

Christopher walked over and saw a jar full of pens and pencils. He picked one out, noticing a framed photograph of a young woman.

"Is that your daughter?" he asked George.

George chuckled. "No, that's a picture of my wife. It was taken right after we got married."

Christopher realized he should have known it was an old picture now that he looked at it more closely. Nobody wore their hair like that anymore.

"You'd better grab another piece of candy on your way here," George suggested. "You can grab a butterscotch for me too while you're at it."

Christopher did as he was told and then handed George his piece of candy before joining him on the sofa.

"Okay, question one," Christopher began, laying his paper on the coffee table. "Did you like being a soldier in World War II?"

"Well, now, that's an interesting question." George slowly unwrapped his butterscotch candy. "I liked my army buddies a lot. They hailed from all over the country and became some of my best friends."

Christopher wrote as fast as he could, trying to get down everything George was saying. He realized too late that he should have brought a tape recorder with him.

"I liked seeing different parts of the world," George continued. "I didn't like being away from home or fighting people I'd never met before."

Christopher finished jotting down the answer and then moved on to the next question. "What day do you remember most?"

George thought about it for a long time. "There are a lot of days I remember. Some good and some bad. I remember landing in France on D-Day. It was . . ." His voice trailed off, and he cleared his throat. "War may be necessary sometimes, Christopher, but it's always horrible. A lot of good men died that day."

"Were you ever hurt?" Christopher asked.

"I got shot in the leg during one battle, but it was just a flesh wound. The medic was able to stop the bleeding and wrap it up for me so I could stay with my unit."

Christopher looked up from his paper. "Didn't you want to go to the hospital so you could get away from all the fighting?"

George shook his head. "I wanted to stay with my buddies. I knew they needed me, and I didn't want to let them down. During a war, your life is in the hands of the men around you. We really depended on each other."

Christopher thought about Dylan waiting for him by the lilac bush, just in case something happened. He wondered if war was kind of like that. "Do you ever talk to any of your army buddies anymore?"

George sighed. "I'm afraid most of them have passed away. We used to exchange letters though, and we held a reunion once or twice. It was nice to see the boys again."

Christopher looked at his list of questions, realizing George had answered many of them already. "What did you miss the most while you were in the army?"

George smiled at the question. "That's an easy one. My Helen. You've seen her picture. Wasn't she a looker?"

Christopher smiled back at him. It was hard to imagine a man as old as George being in love with somebody.

"She passed away a couple of years ago," George continued. "I miss her every day."

"Was she in the USO?" Christopher asked, remembering his grandma talking about it.

"Sure she was. She planted a huge victory garden too, with plenty of vegetables for all the neighbors."

"My sister planted a victory garden a couple of weeks ago. It has strawberries and bok choy and a bunch of other things."

"My Helen planted something else too. Do you want to see it?"

"Sure," Christopher said. He followed him out the back door, expecting George to point out a tree. Instead, George walked over to the rosebush that Christopher had accidentally set on fire.

"Helen planted a yellow rosebush right after I left for basic training. She called it her victory rosebush and looked at it whenever she missed me."

"So it's like . . . eighty years old?"

George chuckled. "Not quite. Helen took some cuttings from the first rosebush and planted a second one. Then she took cuttings from that bush and planted a third one. She kept doing that all these years, right up until she died."

"Wow," Christopher said, feeling about as low as the worm crawling on his shoe.

"I guess you could say this rosebush is the great-great-great-grandchild of that first victory rose. That's why it has a special place in my heart."

Christopher could see the singe marks on some of the leaves and branches of the bush. He wanted to tell George he was sorry for burning his special victory rosebush, but he was too afraid of what his reaction might be.

"You okay, Christopher?" George asked. "You seem kind of quiet."

"Yeah, I'm okay," Christopher said, folding up his paper and stuffing it back in his pocket. "But I'd better get going. Grandma will be expecting me for supper soon."

"Well, thank you for listening to my stories," George told him. "Come back any time."

"Thanks for the interview," Christopher said, practically running from the yard.

He didn't want to face the rosebush anymore or George Kimball either. He didn't want to face what he'd done.

CHARLOTTE LOOKED UP from her cookbook as Emily walked into the house after school. There were tears running down her granddaughter's face. "Emily, what's wrong?"

"This," she cried, opening her backpack and pulling a crumpled sheet of paper from it. She tossed it on the kitchen table and then sank down into a chair.

Charlotte moved next to her and smoothed out the paper. "Oh dear." Someone had Photoshopped a picture of Emily's face onto an ugly orange prom dress. They'd also printed the words "The Prom Queen of Liars."

"Where did this come from?" Charlotte asked her.

"Nicole, of course." Emily sniffed. "She taped it on my locker sometime during school today after telling everybody that I lied about going to the prom and the party."

"What a mean, silly thing to do," Charlotte said, irritated with Nicole. "I'm going to call her mother."

"No, Grandma!" Emily cried. "You can't do that. It would only make things worse."

"Then I'm going to call the principal," she said, her irritation evolving into anger. "This behavior has got to stop."

"Please don't call *anybody*. I did what you said and just ignored her. It was awful, but at least Nicole didn't have the pleasure of seeing me cry." Fresh tears pooled in Emily's eyes. "I waited until I got home."

Charlotte reached out to hug her, wishing she could make her feel better. She'd been ready to hand out a harsh punishment for Emily sneaking out on Saturday night, but it seemed the girl was being punished enough. "I'm so sorry, Emily."

"I just want this stupid prom stuff to be over. I wish Troy had never asked me."

Charlotte smoothed her hair for several minutes, not saying anything as Emily hugged her. Sometimes silence could heal the pain better than words.

"It's not Troy's fault that Nicole doesn't have better manners," Charlotte said at last. "It was a spiteful thing to do, and I'm sure most of the students think much worse of Nicole than they do of you."

She leaned back to look at her. "Really?"

"Really. Her parents would be so embarrassed if they knew what she'd done. I still think I should tell them..."

"No, Grandma," Emily interjected. "I'm not going to let her call me a tattletale too. I'll just keep pretending it doesn't bother me, and maybe she'll leave me alone."

Charlotte gently wiped the tears off Emily's cheeks. "I'm so proud of you for taking the high road."

Emily sniffed. "Proud enough not to punish me for trying to sneak out on Saturday night?"

Charlotte tried not to smile. "I'm afraid that can't go unpunished. How about if you help me get the house clean for Sam's graduation reception this weekend?"

Emily looked surprised. "That's it? That's my punishment?"

"It's a big job," Charlotte told her. "Dusting and vacuuming both upstairs and down."

"That's okay," Emily said. "I want to help."

"Good. I'll make a cleaning list, and you can start tonight."

Emily took a deep breath. "Nicole really is a pain."

"I know," Charlotte agreed. "I'm just so glad she's somebody else's pain."

That made Emily laugh. "Troy said he wouldn't date her if she were the only girl in the high school. He's the one who tore down the poster she put on my locker."

Charlotte was beginning to like Troy more and more. "Good for him. Loyalty is an important trait in a boyfriend."

"I know. He felt so bad for me that he promised to take me out for a special date. I get to choose where and when."

"That sounds nice. What are you going to choose?"

"I don't know yet. I told him I'll have to think about it."

Charlotte rose from the table. "Cleaning gives you a lot of time to think. I'd better make up that list so you can get started."

Emily stood up and hugged her. "Thanks, Grandma. I feel a lot better. I'm going to run upstairs to change clothes."

"All right," Charlotte said, watching her turn and head down the hall. She finally had her old Emily back and thanked God that her granddaughter wasn't mean-spirited like Nicole Evans.

"Lord, please bless Emily," Charlotte prayed aloud, "and bless Nicole too. She's a troublemaker, Lord, but You know her heart. Help all of us to remember to love one another. Amen."

Chapter Nineteen

"This really stinks."

Sam looked up from his sweeping to see Paul on his hands and knees scraping a piece of gum off one of the bleacher seats. It was a rainy Tuesday, and the day felt as gloomy as Sam's mood. He hated detention. "Do you want to trade jobs?"

"Oh, yeah," Paul replied, "I really want to sweep up all the junk that the junior-high kids leave behind after gym class. Do you know I actually found a dirty diaper in these bleachers? How gross is that?"

"I'm sure no junior-high kid left it there," Jake told him from his perch on top of the ladder. He was painting the chipped spots in the wall above the gym door.

"Well, somebody did." Paul tossed something to Sam. "Here, catch."

Sam cried out and jumped away from the object as it fell in front of him. Then he leaned down to take a closer look. "That's not a diaper. It's an old, white T-shirt."

Paul was doubled over with laughter. "I really got you, Slater. It serves you right for having a wicked witch for an aunt."

Sam ignored him and picked up his broom again. Paul had been making remarks like that about Dana ever since their detention started a week ago. All they had to do was make it through their last day of detention, and they'd be home free.

"How does this look?" Jake called out to them. "Did I miss any spots?"

"Right there." Paul pointed toward him.

"Where?" Jake asked, looking at the wall. "I don't see anything."

"That bare spot right in the back of your head." Paul grinned. "Oh, wait a minute, that doesn't need paint. It needs a toupee."

"Ignore him," Sam told Jake, shaking his head at Paul's silly antics. He wanted to finish the job Dana had assigned them and then leave in time for his job at the airport. He was grateful to Ed Haffner for giving him another chance and didn't want to be late.

Jake reached up to feel the back of his head, not realizing he had wet paint on his fingers. "I don't have a bald spot, do I?"

"No," Sam replied, "but now you have white paint in your hair."

Paul started laughing again. "Man, you guys are so gullible. I'm not sure you're ready to graduate and go out into the big, bad world."

"I'm sure we'll manage," Sam said wryly.

He pushed the broom across the floor and swept the debris into a pile that had been building since he first started sweeping the gym floor. He couldn't wait until tomorrow. All the seniors would check out of their lockers around noon and then get organized to leave for their senior trip. After all the work he'd done in the last week at school and at the airport, and with the extra chores at home, Sam really needed this fun getaway.

"I'm sick of this," Paul announced, walking down the bleacher steps. "If Mrs. Stevenson wants the bleachers any cleaner she can do it herself. That's probably all she's good for anyway."

"Hey, Paul," Sam called out to him. "Shut it. Let's just get this done."

Paul walked over to him. "You're sticking up for your aunt after what she did to us? She could have let it go, you know. No one would have been any wiser. It was just a bunch of stupid beach balls."

"Well, she didn't, so just drop it," Sam said, shaking the broom out above the debris pile.

"Make me!" Paul said, dropping into a wrestling pose. He grinned as he bounced around Sam. "Come on, Slater. Let's see what you got."

"Quit goofing around," Jake said. "We're already in enough trouble."

"Are you chicken, Sam?" Paul teased, lightly jabbing him in the chest with his hand. "Are you afraid scary Aunt Dana might find out?"

"Get out of my way," Sam told him, losing patience with his friend.

"Make me," Paul prodded, still acting like he wanted to wrestle.

"If I wanted to, I could take you down."

Paul jabbed at him again. "It's all talk until you show me. Come on, we might as well have a little fun on our last day of detention."

Sam ignored him, reaching for the dustpan. Just as he was about to scrape the debris into it, Paul kicked at the pile, sending dust and debris everywhere.

"What did you do that for?" Sam cried, throwing down the dustpan.

"You can finish cleaning after we wrestle—unless you're afraid of the wicked witch of Bedford High. Mrs. Stevenson could fly in on her broomstick any moment and make us clean the warts off her face."

"Leave my Aunt Dana out of this."

Paul jabbed at his chest a third time and then a fourth. "Make me, Sam. Make me."

"That's it," Sam said, giving him a shove.

Paul slid backward on the slick gym floor and then lost his balance and fell to the ground. Sam jumped on top of him and pinned his shoulders to the floor. "Looks like I can take you down after all."

"Sam!" Dana's voice echoed in the gym. She stood on the other side of the gym inside one of the smaller doorways.

"Uh-oh," Paul groaned. "Now we're in for it."

"Let me handle this," Sam told him. He pulled himself off of Paul and rose to his feet. "I'm sorry about that, Aunt Dana. You see . . ."

"In my office, Sam," Dana demanded. "Right now."

Dana stood in the doorway while Sam walked past her and headed to her office.

"I can't believe you were starting a fight during your detention," Dana told him. "I thought you knew better than that, Sam."

He didn't say anything, aware that blaming Paul would only lead to both of them getting into trouble. He thought about the war letters from his Great-Grandpa Les and how he talked about sticking by his buddies through thick and thin. Paul might be annoying at times, very annoying, but Sam knew he was just goofing around.

"Well?" Dana asked. "What do you have to say for yourself?"

He shrugged. "Nothing, I guess."

She stared at him. "That's it? Give me something to work with here, Sam."

He wasn't about to tell her the things Paul had said about her. That would only hurt her feelings and get Paul into even more trouble. "Paul said something I didn't like, so I shoved him. End of story."

"When I came in, you were on top of him."

Sam shrugged again. "Yeah, I guess so."

Dana shook her head. "Fighting is against the school rules, but you'll be done with school tomorrow so I can't give you more detention."

Sam breathed a sigh of relief. He'd been afraid that Dana would make him come back to school after the seniors were released.

"That doesn't leave me any choice," Dana continued, "but to ban you from the senior trip."

Sam's heart dropped to his toes. He'd been looking forward to that senior trip. He *needed* that senior trip. But the expression on Dana's face right now told him that it wouldn't do any good to argue with her.

"Did you hear me?" she asked him.

"I heard you," Sam replied, still reeling at the punishment she'd given him. "Can I go now?"

"Yes," she said softly. "You may go."

A few minutes later, Paul and Jake met him out in the parking lot.

"What happened?" Jake asked.

Sam opened his car door. "I'm banned from the senior trip."

"No way!" Jake exclaimed. "Are you serious?"

"Yep," Sam replied. "We're almost done with school, so that was the only punishment she could give me. I guess you guys will have to have fun without me."

"Sam, I'm sorry," Paul said, looking genuinely contrite. "It's my fault . . ."

"Forget it," Sam told him. "There's no reason for two of us to miss the senior trip. Just promise you'll tell me all about it when you get back."

"This stinks," Paul said.

"Yeah." Sam climbed into his car. "It does."

THAT EVENING when Pete got home from the farm, Dana told him what had happened at school.

"You banned him from the senior trip?" Pete whistled low. "Man, that's harsh."

Dana pulled a warm plate for Pete out of the oven and set it on the placemat in front of him. "I didn't have any choice, Pete. Sam had no excuse for fighting, and that was the only punishment I could give him."

Pete pulled the foil off his plate and then picked up his fork. "I just feel bad for the kid. I remember what it was like hearing how much fun everybody had on the senior trip when I didn't get to go."

"I know." Dana slipped into the chair next to him. She'd barely eaten two bites of her own supper, finally placing most of her meatloaf in a plastic container to take for lunch tomorrow. "I feel bad for him too."

"I got over it," Pete said, scooping up a forkful of meatloaf.

"I'm sure Sam will too. He's still got graduation to look forward to this weekend."

"I'm so glad I turned down the job of assistant principal." Dana leaned back in her chair, feeling more relaxed now that she'd shared her troubles with her husband. "I'll put in my time the rest of this year because Principal Duncan asked me to fill in, but I hate handing out punishments to the students, especially when I get the feeling the kids aren't telling me everything."

Pete chuckled. "Of course they aren't telling you everything. They know better than to snitch on one of their classmates."

"Well, that makes it really hard to be fair."

"I'm sure you're as fair as you can be," he said, leaning over to kiss the tip of her nose. "And you make a great meatloaf. It tastes just like Mom's."

She laughed. "That's because I got the recipe from her. I know the way to my man's heart."

"That you do." Pete speared another chunk of meatloaf with his fork. "And don't worry about Sam. Before you know it, this thing will all blow over."

Dana took comfort in his words that night, but the next morning she wasn't so sure. Sam passed her in the hallway without speaking to her or meeting her gaze. No doubt he was mad about the senior trip; she just hoped he didn't stay mad for long. It occurred to her that she could have asked Principal Duncan to handle it, but that seemed like passing the buck. She was the one who had seen Sam shove Paul and jump on top of him when he was down.

When she reached her office, Dana walked inside and tried to put her trouble with Sam out of her mind. She had a lot she wanted to accomplish today.

She set her file folders on top of her desk and then sat

down and started looking through her planner to prepare for the day.

"Mrs. Stevenson?"

Dana looked up to see Paul Marshall standing in the doorway. "Yes, Paul?"

"If you're not too busy, I'd like to talk to you for a minute."

Dana glanced at the clock, noting that the first bell wouldn't ring for another fifteen minutes. Since Paul's detention was over she could guess why he was here.

"Come in," she told him. "Is it about Sam?"

"Yes, ma'am." Paul walked over to her desk. "The thing is . . . what you saw in the gym yesterday was my fault. Sam had nothing to do with it."

"I know what I saw, Paul," she said gently, admiring the boy for standing up for his friend. "Sam shoved you and then pinned you on the ground."

"But you don't know why he shoved me or why he pinned me down." Paul took a deep breath. "See, I'd been complaining . . . about you. Calling you a witch and stuff."

Dana saw his face redden as he spoke, but she didn't say anything.

"I'm really sorry about that, Mrs. Stevenson. Sam kept telling me to stop, but I was tired of cleaning and ready to goof around. I challenged him to wrestle me, but he just kept sweeping. I started jabbing him and saying he was afraid of his witchy aunt."

Now the boy's face was so beet-red that Dana was starting to feel sorry for him. She knew teenage boys well enough to assume he wasn't the first one to call her a witch, nor would he be the last. It came with the territory. "Go on."

"Anyway, I kept making fun of him, saying he was chicken and stuff for not wrestling with me. I kept jabbing him; then

I kicked at the pile of stuff he'd swept just to get him riled up."

"I'd say it worked," Dana said wryly. "Is that when he shoved you?"

Paul shook his head. "No, you don't understand. He didn't shove me until I said something about you again. I made some smart remark about you flying into the gym on your broomstick, and that's when he gave me a push. He was defending you, Mrs. Stevenson, 'cause you're his aunt and stuff."

Dana was surprised to hear the whole story and wondered why Sam hadn't told her. Then she remembered that students didn't rat each other out.

"I'm sure he didn't mean for me to fall down," Paul continued, "but once I did, I guess he thought the only way to stop me from yammering at him was to prove that he could pin me. That's when you walked in."

"I see," Dana said.

Paul squared his shoulders. "So, I think if you're going to ban somebody from the senior trip, it should be me. It was my fault from start to finish, not Sam's."

"Thank you, Paul," Dana said at last, "for telling me what really happened."

"You're welcome," Paul said, his shoulders sagging with relief. "And I'm sorry again about calling you a witch and stuff. You're not really that bad."

She tried not to smile at the backhanded compliment. "You'd better get to class now," she told him. "The bell's about to ring."

"Okay," he said, looking eager to make his escape.

When he was gone, Dana folded her hands together and prayed for guidance. "Dear Lord," she whispered, "what do I do now?"

Chapter Twenty

"Can you believe this is the last time we'll eat lunch here?"

Sam sat in the school cafeteria with Paul and Jake, marveling at the fact that he'd never be faced with eating the school cook's "tuna surprise" again.

"It does feel a little weird," Jake agreed. "Today is the last day of classes too. I'll never have to sit through one of Mr. Mason's boring history lectures again."

Sam grinned. "You'll still have to sit through boring history lectures in college."

"Yeah, but college is different," Jake said. "We'll be on our own, without our parents there telling us what to do. I hear the college professors don't get on your case either. If you don't study or come to class, they just flunk you."

Paul shook his head. "And you think that's a good thing?"

"To not have teachers breathing down my neck all the time?" Jake said. "That sounds good to me."

Sam noticed that neither of the boys had mentioned the senior trip. Although he was still upset about it, he wanted them to have a good time.

"So are you packed for Lincoln?" Sam asked them. "The bus is leaving this afternoon. I heard one of the girls say you're going to stop at the burger joint in Harding to pick up supper."

"I'm not sure I'm going," Paul said.

Sam couldn't believe his ears. "Why not?"

"Because of what happened yesterday," Paul explained. "It's not fair for me to go and you to stay in Bedford. We both know it's my fault."

"You're talking crazy," Sam told him, eager to convince Paul to change his mind. "I fell on the grenade for you. The least you can do is go to Lincoln and have a great time. That's what I want you to do."

Paul shook his head. "Sorry, but I still don't think it's right."

Jake looked between his two friends. "How am I supposed to have fun if you're both here in Bedford? I might as well stay here too. Then we can make our own fun."

"I think I've had enough of making our own fun for a while," Sam said, remembering their foiled prank. "You guys *have* to go to Lincoln. Seriously, I'll be mad if you don't go because of me."

The loud speaker in the cafeteria crackled, which was always a prelude to an announcement. "Sam Slater, please come to the office."

"Are you kidding me?" Sam said, wondering what he was in trouble for now.

"Sam Slater," the speaker repeated, "please come to the office."

"Just think," Jake said. "After today you'll never be called to the office again."

Sam wasn't so sure. The way his luck was going, Principal Duncan would tell him he'd flunked one of his classes and would have to repeat the year.

Although he really didn't think that was possible, Sam

knew that coming back to Bedford High for any reason wasn't an option. He'd join the army first, like he'd thought of doing a few months ago. Anything to get him out of high school.

Sam walked into the office and was surprised to see Dana sitting at the secretary's desk. "What are you doing here?"

"I'm covering for the secretary while she's at lunch," Dana told him. "It's part of the assistant principal's duties."

Along with ruining all my fun, Sam thought to himself. "So you called me in here?"

"That's right. Have a seat."

Sam took the nearest chair, hoping this wouldn't take long. The lunch hour would be over soon, and he didn't want to waste it hearing how Dana was disappointed in his behavior. Or maybe she wanted to grill him about the incident with Paul yesterday. Maybe Principal Duncan had told her the punishment wasn't harsh enough.

Sam waited in silence, expecting the worst.

Instead, Dana surprised him. "Sam," she began, "I want to apologize to you."

"What for?"

"For thinking the worst about what happened yesterday. I've learned from another student that it didn't unfold the way I previously thought."

Sam stared at her, not certain what to say. Obviously, Paul or Jake had told her what really happened. But why would they do that and risk losing the senior trip themselves? Then he remembered their conversation in the cafeteria.

"Paul told you, didn't he?" Sam said.

"I'm not comfortable revealing private conversations with other students. Let's just say the whole story came out."

Even though she wouldn't name Paul, Sam had no doubt he was who she meant. Now Sam really did want to wrestle him to the ground. The big dummy had put his chance to go on the senior trip at risk because of a guilty conscience.

"You've got to let Paul go on the senior trip," Sam implored. "We were just goofing around yesterday. It was my fault all this happened. I was the one who shoved him."

"That's not the story I heard."

"It's what happened," he insisted.

"So you weren't trying to defend me?"

Sam's cheeks warmed. "Paul didn't really mean what he said about you. Sometimes he gets carried away."

"I know. He already apologized to me more than once." Dana folded her hands on her desk. "But that brings me back to the reason I called you in here. I need to apologize to you."

Now Sam was really confused. "I don't understand."

"I'm not surprised," Dana told him. "The fact that you're my nephew now makes it all rather complicated. I think I was trying to prove that I wasn't showing favoritism to you, but I ended up going too far in the other direction."

"You mean the week-long detention?"

"Well, that was probably justified," Dana told him. "Principal Duncan agreed with me on it. But I overreacted when I saw you and Paul scuffling yesterday. Once I heard the full story, I realized that."

Sam tried not to get his hopes up, but he couldn't help it. "So that's why you called me in here? To apologize?"

She smiled. "To apologize and to tell you that you'd better get ready for the senior trip. I hear it's going to be a pretty fun time."

Sam jumped out of his chair. "All right!"

Dana laughed, even as she put a finger to her lips. "Don't make too much noise. You still have to be good for the next few hours so we don't have to go through this again."

"I'll be so good you won't even recognize me," Sam promised her. "Thanks, Aunt Dana. I can't wait to tell Paul and Jake that I can go to Lincoln with them. Then I better call Grandma and ask her to bring my stuff."

"You'd better get moving," she urged. "Lunchtime is almost over."

Sam left the office, resisting the urge to jump up and touch the ceiling. He'd meant what he said in that office. For the last few hours of his time at Bedford High, Sam Slater would be a model student.

"IT'S TIME FOR OUR HISTORY LESSON," Miss Luka told the sixth-grade class, "and we're going to do something fun today."

Christopher glanced over at Dylan with a grin, hoping they'd get to play a game. Sometimes, they split into two teams and played history quiz bowl. Miss Luka would ask questions about whatever they'd been studying in history class. Each correct answer was worth five points, and the team with the most points at the end of the game got a special treat. Last time they'd played, the winners got extra free time during class.

He and Dylan had both been on the losing team, but Christopher had been reading all of his history lessons since then, determined to be on the winning team the next time they played.

"Do we get to play quiz bowl?" Liza Cummings asked.

"Not today," Miss Luka replied, provoking groans from the class. "Instead, we're going to have a special guest. His name is . . ." A knock at the classroom door interrupted Miss Luka. She smiled and said, "Here he is."

Everyone turned around to see who would walk through the door. To Christopher's surprise, he saw George Kimball walk into the classroom, his cane tapping on the linoleum floor.

"Oh, great," Dylan mumbled under his breath. He sank down in his chair, his gaze fixed on the top of his desk.

"Class, this is Mr. George Kimball," Miss Luka said. "He's the World War II veteran that Christopher interviewed for the school newspaper. When he called to tell me what a fine young man Christopher was, I invited him to come and speak to our class."

Christopher blushed at the compliment as several of his classmates turned to look at him. Christopher was sure if they knew what he'd done no one would call him a fine young man, least of all Uncle George.

"Christopher, why don't you come up here and give Mr. Kimball a proper introduction," Miss Luka said. "You can tell us some of the things you learned during the interview."

Stifling a sigh, Christopher rose from his chair and approached the front of the class. George beamed at him, patting his shoulder when Christopher stood beside him.

Christopher cleared his throat and then began to speak. "I learned that Uncle George, I mean, Mr. Kimball . . ."

"That's all right, Christopher," George interjected. "You and the rest of the class can call me Uncle George. No need to stand on formalities among friends."

"Okay," Christopher said, wishing George wasn't so nice. It only made him feel worse about burning his rosebush. "Uncle George told me all about his experiences in World War II. He had to leave for basic training right after he was married and didn't see his wife again until the war was over."

"I still have all the letters she wrote me," George told the class. "We didn't have cell phones or e-mail back then, so my wife would write long letters to me every week. In the summer, she'd place petals from our yellow rosebush in the letters. She called it our victory rosebush, and I still think of her whenever I smell roses."

"George made a lot of good friends during the war," Christopher said quickly, wanting to change the subject from the victory rose. "He also fought during D-Day."

Christopher struggled to think of something else to mention, something other than the victory bush, but his mind was blank. George was smiling down at him, which only made him feel worse.

Miss Luka stepped forward. "Does anyone have a question for Mr. Kimball?"

Christopher breathed a sigh of relief as several hands shot up in the air. Miss Luka pointed to Natalie Johnson, who sat in the front row.

"Did people shoot at you?" Natalie asked.

"They sure did," George said. "As a soldier you learn pretty fast to stay low and not call attention to your position."

Justin Taylor asked the next question. "Were you ever shot?"

George nodded. "I took a bullet in the leg. It wasn't too serious, so I got to stay with my unit."

"Did you win any medals?" Rachel Wells asked after Miss Luka called on her.

George grew quiet for a moment and then slowly nodded his head. "I got a Purple Heart after my injury."

"You never told me that," Christopher blurted out before he could stop himself. Why hadn't he asked George that question during the interview? Since he hadn't written his final draft yet, he figured there was still time to add these new details.

George turned to Christopher. "It's not something I talk about much. I didn't really do anything special to win that medal. We lost a lot of good men in battle; some of them were buddies of mine." He paused a moment to gather himself. "But standing here today, I know those great sacrifices were worth it to keep you and the rest of your classmates living in freedom."

Christopher wanted to sink into the floor. George, the war hero, had fought for him. And what had Christopher done? Burned his rosebush and kept it a secret from him.

Christopher felt so guilty that he barely heard the rest of the questions his classmates asked. Before he knew it, Miss Luka was thanking George for visiting the class and the students were all applauding.

As Miss Luka escorted George to the door, Christopher walked back to his desk and sat down. He felt sick to his stomach.

"He didn't recognize me," Dylan whispered to him. "I think we're in the clear."

"We've got to tell him what we did," Christopher whispered in return.

"Are you crazy?"

"I don't want to lie to George anymore. He's a war hero, and he called me his friend."

Dylan shook his head in disgust. "Yeah, well, if you tell him we bombed his rosebush, you won't be his friend anymore. He'll hate you."

Christopher didn't say anything, fearing that Dylan was right. If he confessed the truth about the rosebush, George would hate him. If he kept it a secret, Christopher would hate himself. It was a battle he simply couldn't win.

Chapter Twenty-One

"I brought cream puffs to celebrate the fact that it's finally Friday."

Charlotte watched Dana set the plate of cream puffs on the kitchen table. "They look delicious, but you know I'm on a diet, don't you?"

"Yes, but Grandma Maxie made them and insisted I bring them out to you." Dana hung her purse on a chair. "Besides, we'll probably work off the calories by the time we finish decorating for Sam's graduation."

Charlotte smiled, wishing it were that easy. Grandma Maxie's cream puffs did look delicious. Maybe she'd treat herself to one, and only one, when they were done getting the house ready for Sam's graduation reception.

"How about a glass of iced tea before we get started?" Charlotte asked.

"That sounds great." Dana pulled out a chair and sat down. "I went into school early today to catch up on paperwork, so I'm a little tired. A glass of tea will be the perfect pick-me-up."

Charlotte retrieved a pitcher of tea from the refrigerator and poured a glass for each of them.

"How are you doing on your diet?" Dana asked her.

"As of today, I've lost four pounds." Charlotte set the glasses on the table and sat down. "Which isn't bad considering all the problems I've had to deal with lately. I'm not sure if it's spring fever or just teen fever, but those grandkids of mine seem to be attracting trouble this month."

Dana sighed. "I know exactly what you mean. I think I'm even more excited for the school year to be over than the students are. I can't wait to go back to being just a teacher again."

Charlotte took a sip of her tea. "Well, I think you've done a fine job filling in for the assistant principal. I was impressed with how you handled things with Sam."

Dana nodded. "I definitely learned a lesson about not jumping to conclusions. Looks like the students aren't the only ones getting an education at Bedford High."

Charlotte chuckled, pleased that everything had turned out all right. "Well, Sam had a wonderful time on his senior trip. He couldn't stop talking about it when he got home last night."

"Where is Sam?" Dana asked. "I didn't see his car in the driveway."

"He's working late tonight so he can have the weekend off. I'm not sure it's really hit him yet that he'll be graduating from high school tomorrow. It hasn't hit me either."

"Do you know if Kevin is coming?"

"We haven't heard a word from him. I even tried sending him an e-mail the other day just to confirm he was coming, but he never responded."

Dana frowned. "Why would he do that? Surely he could at least politely decline the invitation."

"I'm not sure why he does anything." Charlotte curled her hands around the cold glass. "The strange thing is that

Sam hasn't said anything about Kevin coming to his graduation since the day he asked me to invite him."

"Maybe he knows not to get his hopes up."

"Maybe," Charlotte echoed, not certain that was the reason. "I was going to talk to him about it, but Bob suggested we let Sam come to us if he wants to talk. I don't want to make a big deal out of it if Kevin doesn't show up."

"What about Emily and Christopher?" Dana asked. "Are they looking forward to seeing him?"

"I don't think Emily cares too much one way or the other. It's hard for me to tell what Christopher's thinking. I don't want to play what-ifs with them about Kevin until we know whether he's coming tomorrow. I figure we can deal with the fallout later, just like we've done before."

"I can't imagine missing my own child's high school graduation."

"Neither can I. But look how much of their lives he's already missed. I thought that might change when he showed up in December, but he seems to have disappeared again."

"Those poor kids. It just goes to show what a great job you and Bob have done with them. All three seem pretty happy and healthy to me."

Charlotte smiled. "I feel that way most days, but on other days . . . Let's just say that it never gets boring around here."

Dana reached for the plate of cream puffs and pulled back the plastic wrap. "Want one?"

"No thanks. I'll wait a while."

Dana picked up a cream puff. "Where are Emily and Christopher?"

"Emily's doing some cleaning for Lydia Middleton tonight, and Christopher is in the family room rewriting his story for the school newspaper. I think this must be his third draft already. He interviewed George Kimball, a World War II veteran, and the two of them have become good pals. In fact, I told Christopher to extend an invitation to the USO dance to him, but I don't know if he'll follow through or not."

"I can't wait to read his story." Dana took a bite of her cream puff. "Mmm, these are amazing." Then she winced. "Oops, sorry. I shouldn't say that to someone on a diet."

"They do look tempting," Charlotte said. "But I promised myself I wouldn't cheat anymore. There's only a week left until Memorial Weekend, so I can surely resist temptation for that long."

"How's Bob doing on his diet?"

Charlotte shrugged. "I don't know. He decided not to weigh himself anymore after that first time. He said he'll be able to tell how he's doing by how his clothes fit him."

"Well, that's probably true." Dana licked some whipped cream off her thumb. "Has he tried on Les's old uniform again?"

"Not yet. He's going to wait until next week." Charlotte took another sip of her tea. "I hope it fits him. He wants to wear it so badly."

"I wish I could convince Pete to join the rest of them in the reenactment. He's just so overwhelmed with all the work he has to do right now he can barely make time to come to Sam's graduation tomorrow."

"Any luck convincing him to ask Bob for help?"

Dana shook head. "To tell you the truth, I've quit trying for a while. I'm hoping the things I've said already will start to sink in."

"Sometimes that's the best strategy," Charlotte said, remembering when she'd done the same with Bob. Most people didn't like to be pushed into changing their minds; they had to do it on their own.

Dana popped the last bit of cream puff into her mouth. "I feel much better now. Where do we start decorating?"

Charlotte rose from her chair. "I thought we'd start in the living room since most of the guests will come through the front door. Then we can decorate down the hallway and into the kitchen. I'm going to serve the food and cake in here."

"That's a good idea. What are you making?"

"Some cold lunch meat sandwiches and a variety of salads. Nothing too fancy." She walked over to the counter to retrieve some of the decorations. "Graduation is at two o'clock tomorrow afternoon, so there should be enough food to carry people over to supper."

"It sounds to me like enough food to count as supper, especially with cake for dessert. Are you baking that yourself or having someone else do it?"

"Hannah offered to bake and decorate a cake for Sam. She's really quite good at cake decorating. She took a class once in Harding and picked up the techniques very quickly."

"What have you got there?" Dana asked, walking over to take a look.

"I've got blue and white streamers," Charlotte said, pulling the crepe-paper rolls out of the sack. "And some of that shiny confetti that you sprinkle on tables."

"Oh, cute!" Dana exclaimed, taking one of the packets of colorful confetti out of the sack along with some rolls of adhesive tape. "The confetti is cut into little graduation caps and diplomas and stars."

Charlotte chuckled. "I'm sure they'll be a mess to clean up off the floor once the reception is over, but I'll worry about that later."

"What's this?" Dana asked, pulling a thick scroll of paper out of the sack.

"Open it," Charlotte told her, grabbing one end of the scroll so Dana could unroll it.

"Congratulations, Graduate," Dana read as she walked backward to unroll the scroll. "It has Sam's graduation picture on it. How did you do that?"

"I ordered it at a store in Harding that specializes in personalized banners and signs," Charlotte said. "Julia Benson told me about it. I hope Sam likes it. That was his favorite senior picture."

"I'm sure he'll love it," Dana said. "Where shall we put it?"

"How about the living room wall opposite the picture window? That way everyone can see it when they come in the house."

"Perfect," Dana said, carrying the banner and a roll of tape into the living room.

Charlotte followed with the sack of decorations. "Thank you for coming out to help me tonight. I think this is going to be even more fun than I thought."

"You know what they say." Dana tore some tape from the roll and attached it to a back corner of the banner. "Many hands make light work."

Charlotte helped Dana position the banner on the wall. "If only we could get our husbands to start living by that motto again."

"They'll be together most of the day tomorrow," Dana said. "Maybe that will help."

Charlotte hoped so. She didn't want those two to continue this way all summer. There was simply too much to do on the farm, and Bob and Pete knew that even better than she did.

Many hands make light work. The motto echoed in her head as she and Dana put up the graduation decorations. Maybe she needed to embroider that on a pair of pillow cases and give one to her husband and one to her son. That might be the only way to get the message through their thick heads.

SAM WALKED INTO Bedford High School for the last time on Saturday afternoon. It was a little before one o'clock, and the seniors were supposed to gather in the band room to get ready for graduation. He carried his graduation robe on a plastic hanger slung over his shoulder as he walked down the hallway. His grandma had insisted on ironing it the night before to get all the wrinkles out.

To his surprise, Sam felt a little nervous. He'd barely been able to eat lunch and now his stomach flip-flopped when he opened the door to the band room and saw some of his classmates already putting on their robes.

"Slater!" Jake walked over to him, his black robe flowing behind him as he raised his hand for a high five.

Sam slapped hands with him, unable to stop the grin spreading across his face. "Can you believe we're really doing this?"

Jake looked down at his robe. "Now that I've got this thing on, I'm ready to believe it."

"Where are the caps?" Sam asked, looking around the room. He saw that some of the students were already wearing them.

"Over by the piano. Mrs. Stevenson is handing them out."

Sam took his robe off the hanger and then slipped it on, zipping it up the front. "How do I look?"

Jake grinned. "I'll show you." He pulled a small digital camera out of his pocket and snapped a picture. "See?" he said, holding the camera up for Sam to view the small screen on the back.

"Hey, not bad," Sam said, admiring himself in the photograph. "It's not an outfit I'd want to wear every day, but I do look pretty distinguished."

"Now take a picture of me," Jake said, handing over his camera.

Sam looked at the camera's screen and snapped Jake's picture. He was mentally kicking himself for not borrowing Emily's camera. Hopefully, she'd bring it with her to the graduation ceremony and he could borrow it afterward. "Where's Paul?" Sam asked, handing the camera back to Jake.

"Probably running late as usual. I guess he wants Principal Duncan yelling at him one last time before he leaves Bedford High."

Sam smiled. "Let's go get our graduation caps and beat the rush."

"Lead the way."

Sam headed toward the piano at the back corner of the room. He could see Aunt Dana there, standing by a big box. She looked nice in her light blue dress and even wore a corsage of class flowers, white roses with blue tips.

"Hello, boys," Dana said as he and Jake approached her. "I'd say you have large heads."

"Is that supposed to be a compliment?" Sam asked, a little confused by the comment.

She laughed. "I just meant that you'd need the large-size cap. They come in three sizes, and most of the boys wear a size large."

"Cool," Jake said as she handed a cap to him.

"There are two bobby pins attached to them already," Dana told them, handing a cap to Sam. "You might want to use them if the cap feels like it's going to fall off. Either that or exchange it for another size."

"I've never used a bobby pin before," Jake said, staring at the bobby pins on his cap as if they were radioactive.

"It's no big deal," Sam told him. "Emily uses them all the time."

"Yeah, but she's a girl."

"Why don't you try the caps on," Dana told them. "They might fit just fine without using the bobby pins."

As Sam started to walk away, Dana called him back. "Can I talk to you for a minute?"

"As long as you don't give me detention," he teased.

"Those days are over, thank goodness." Dana turned around and retrieved a small, square present from the shelf behind her. It was wrapped in shiny silver paper with a big, royal blue bow on top.

"Pete and I wanted to give you your graduation gift early, before the ceremony starts."

"Gee, thanks," Sam said, taking it from her. "Should I open it now?"

"Go ahead," she encouraged him.

Sam ripped off the paper and then looked at the picture on the box. His mouth fell open. "You got me a digital camera?"

She smiled. "Pete came up with the idea. He thought you might want a camera of your own now that you're a high school graduate."

Sam wanted to give her a hug, but there were too many people watching. "You're not going to believe it, but I was just wanting one of these."

"Well, I'm glad you like it."

"Are you kidding? I love it!" Sam opened the box and pulled out the sleek silver camera, which was less than an inch thick. "It's small enough for me to carry around in my pocket."

"That's the idea," Dana said. "You'll be much more likely to use it if it's convenient for you to carry. I put batteries in it too, so it's ready to go."

Sam turned on the camera and saw a tiny green light appear on the top. "It's working."

"You can start taking pictures right away."

"Okay." Sam moved to her side and held his arm out in front of him so the camera was pointed at them both. "Smile."

He pressed the button on top, and the camera flashed. Sam turned it around to see the picture on the camera's screen. He and Dana were just a little off center, but they were both smiling.

He showed the screen to Dana. "What do you think?"

"Very nice," Dana said. "I'm honored to be in your first photograph."

"Thanks again," Sam told her, walking away as more students came up to her for their graduation caps. He looked around the room. It was filling up fast, and he'd lost sight of Jake.

"Hey, Sam."

He turned around to find Arielle standing behind him. "Hi there. You look great."

She smiled. "You look nice too."

He held out his arms, creating wings with the sleeves of the graduation gown. "The look is growing on me."

"Can you believe we finally made it?" she said. "I'm so excited!"

"Me too." He held up his camera. "Smile."

She posed for him as he snapped the picture. Sam looked down at the screen. "That's a good one."

"Now let's take one together," Arielle said, moving closer to him. She held her arm out with her camera facing both of them and then snapped a picture. Sam followed her example with his own camera.

"Isn't this fun?" Arielle said, her face flushed with excitement. "The best part is that we'll have all summer to hang out together before we leave for college."

"It'll be great," Sam said, hoping the summer moved slowly. He didn't want to think about them being apart.

Arielle's friends called her away, and Sam finally spotted Jake and Paul in their caps and gowns on the other side of the room.

This is really happening.

Sam's stomach did a flip-flop, knowing that in just a little while they'd be walking into the auditorium to start the ceremony. He wondered if his dad would be there and then decided it didn't really matter to him all that much.

He wasn't going to let anything ruin this day.

Chapter Twenty-Two

Charlotte didn't see Kevin anywhere.

She stood inside the high school auditorium trying to see around the crowds of people milling about. The first few rows were reserved for graduates; the next rows were reserved with the graduates' nameplates for the graduates' families; and the rest of the guests were seated behind the families.

Charlotte walked down the aisle with Emily, finally spotting Sam's name in the sixth row from the front. "It looks like we'll have good seats."

"May I sit in the aisle seat, Grandma?" Emily asked. "Then I can get some good pictures of Sam while they're walking in."

"That's a good idea." Charlotte looked toward the door and saw Bill and his family enter. He was dressed in a suit and holding the baby. Anna had both arms around the two girls, who wore matching blue-gingham dresses with sashes tied in big bows in the back.

"Don't they look cute?" Emily said, waving to get her uncle's attention. "And look at Will. He's wearing a sailor suit."

Charlotte opened her arms as Jennifer and Madison ran up to greet her. "Hello, girls."

"Hi, Grandma," they said in unison.

She gave them each a big hug. "You both look so pretty today."

"Grandma Helen gave us these dresses," Jennifer told her, executing a twirl.

Grandma Helen was Anna's mother and often showered the grandchildren with gifts. Charlotte had given up trying to compete with her a long time ago.

"They're very nice," Charlotte said. "Are you excited to see Sam graduate?"

Madison nodded. "I've never been to a graduation before. Do we get to eat cake?"

Charlotte smiled at the question. "As soon as the graduation ceremony is over, we'll go back to the farm and eat sandwiches and cake."

"May I have the cake first?" Madison asked.

"You'll have to ask your mom and dad," Charlotte told her as Anna and Bill walked up to them.

Charlotte reached out to take the baby from Bill and kissed his chubby cheek. "Hello, Will," she murmured to him. "How's my big boy?"

"He's growing fatter every day," Bill said with a proud smile. "I think Anna feeds him too much."

"He's just a big eater," Anna said. Then she turned to Charlotte. "You look quite nice today."

Charlotte glanced down at her dependable navy blue suit. She'd chosen a pink silk blouse to wear with it. "Thank you, Anna. I like your dress too."

Bill looked around. "Where's Dad?"

"He's over there talking with Hannah and Frank." She searched the room. "And Christopher's around here somewhere." She glanced at her watch. "I know Dana's helping organize the ceremony, but I wonder what's keeping Pete."

"I'm sure he'll be along," Bill said.

Charlotte glanced at her watch. "I'd better go fetch your father. The ceremony is going to start soon." She pointed to the row of seats designated for their family. "We're all sitting over there."

"Almost front-row seats," Bill observed. "We can't complain about that."

While Bill steered his family to their chairs, Charlotte walked over to greet Hannah and Frank.

"There's the proud grandmother," Hannah said. "You look wonderful today, Charlotte. You're practically glowing."

"I'm just so happy this day has finally arrived." She looked up at Bob. "We're both pretty proud of our grandson."

"You have every reason to be," Frank said, tugging on his tie. "I can't wait to get to your place so I can take off this tie. It's been choking me ever since I put it on."

"Oh, Frank," Hannah chided, reaching up to help him, "you probably tied it too tight again."

Bob had worn a suit too, and Charlotte could tell it was a little baggy on him. Maybe his willpower had worked after all and he'd be able to fit into Les's old uniform come Memorial Day.

"We'd better find some seats before they all fill up," Hannah said. "We probably won't see you two after the ceremony. We're going to run back to our place right away so I can pick up Sam's cake."

"Okay," Charlotte said, "we'll see you at our house. The back door is open, so just let yourselves in if we're not there yet."

"Will do," Hannah replied as she and Frank headed toward their seats in the back.

Charlotte could see the graduates starting to line up by the door. "We'd better go sit down too."

"Lead the way," Bob said.

When she reached their row, Charlotte was relieved to see Pete and Christopher sitting on the other side of Bill's family. There were three empty chairs left in the row, two for her and Bob and one reserved for Kevin.

They took their seats, and then Charlotte turned to Bob and whispered, "Kevin's not coming, is he?"

"Doesn't look that way."

The high school band was seated near the stage and started warming up, signaling that the ceremony was about to begin. Emily perched on her chair at the end of the row, her camera at the ready.

"How could Kevin do this to Sam?" Charlotte whispered to her husband. "He didn't even call to tell Sam he couldn't make it."

"That's no surprise, is it?"

That was the saddest part of all to Charlotte. Kevin's absence wasn't a surprise—it was the norm. She supposed there was still a chance he might show up at Heather Creek Farm for the reception, but she doubted it. Kevin had always put himself first, and Sam's graduation seemed to be no exception.

A hush settled over the auditorium as Principal Duncan and the president of the school board took the stage. The principal walked up to the podium.

"Good afternoon," Mr. Duncan began. "It is my privilege to welcome all of you to our commencement ceremony. I know that as the family and friends of these graduates, you have all played a special part in helping them reach this milestone in their lives." He looked toward the entrance and then gave a slight nod. "Now it is my great pleasure to introduce this year's Bedford High School graduates."

Everyone rose as the band began playing "Pomp and Circumstance." Charlotte watched the graduates make the slow processional toward the front of the auditorium, where rows had been cordoned off for them. They walked two at a time up the aisle, one boy and one girl.

Charlotte watched Sam's friend Jake walk by with Arielle next to him, and then Paul followed shortly after them. There were bursts of camera flashes as the seniors walked past their families.

"There he is!" Emily exclaimed, leaning into the aisle with her camera.

Charlotte turned to see Sam heading toward her, his eyes straight ahead and his face solemn as he walked. She could tell he was concentrating on matching the step of the girl beside him. Her throat tightened as he walked by, and she reached out to take Bob's hand. She'd been so busy the last couple of days getting ready for the graduation party that she hadn't really prepared herself for this moment.

When all the graduates had reached the seats, the salutatorian walked up to the stage to give her speech, followed by the class valedictorian. Charlotte soaked up every moment. The ceremony flew by too quickly; before she knew it, the graduates were being called to the stage one by one to receive their diplomas. The principal announced each senior's full name while the president of the school board handed out the diplomas.

Soon, she glimpsed Sam standing in the wings, waiting for his name to be called. Her heart swelled with love and pride.

Charlotte knew the only thing that could make this moment more wonderful would be to have Denise sitting beside her, watching her handsome son receive his diploma.

"Samuel Dillon Slater," the principal announced into the microphone.

Sam strode across the stage and shook hands with the president of the school board as he received his diploma; then he turned slightly for the official photographer to take his picture.

He made it, Denise, Charlotte said silently as tears stung her eyes. *Our boy made it.*

The last student's name was called, and then all the graduates reassembled on the risers on the stage to sing the school song and take one last bow before their families and friends.

After the ceremony, Dana found Pete waiting for her near the front door of the high school.

"There you are," Pete said. "I thought maybe you found a better-looking guy and left without me."

"Very funny," she said, leaning up to give him a kiss on the cheek. "I'm sorry I took so long. I had to make sure the graduates cleared out all their stuff from the band room before I could leave."

"Did Sam like the camera we gave him?"

"He loved it. He was snapping pictures like crazy before the ceremony started."

Dana walked with him to the parking lot. Most of the crowd had cleared out by now, and Principal Duncan would soon be locking the doors to the school. "Wasn't it a lovely ceremony?"

"It seemed a little long to me," Pete replied. "They could have cut those speeches in half and it still would have been too long."

"I thought the speeches were inspiring." Dana took Pete's hand, excited to be spending the rest of the day with her husband. They'd both been so busy they hadn't made much time for each other lately.

"Sam sure looked happy when he got his diploma," Pete said, reaching into his pocket for his car keys.

"You should have seen the kids when they came back to the band room to change out of their robes. They were whooping and hollering and giving each other high fives."

"Probably celebrating the fact that they were finally getting away from mean Mrs. Stevenson," Pete teased.

Dana laughed. "Probably."

When they reached the car, Dana slid into the passenger seat. She unspooled her seatbelt as Pete started the engine.

"Are you ready to head to the farm or do we need to stop by the house first?"

"Let's go to the farm," she replied. "I told your mom I'd help set out the food before all the guests arrive. I just hope I'm not too late. I didn't realize it would take me so long to clear out all the seniors." She smiled. "It seemed like, now that they've graduated, they didn't want to leave the school!"

He laughed as he drove the car out of the parking lot and headed for Heather Creek Road. "Funny how it works that way."

Dana kicked off her heels and leaned back in her seat, taking the chance to relax a little before they reached Heather Creek Farm. "What shall we do after the reception?" she asked him. "Do you want to take in a movie in Harding tonight?"

Pete hesitated. "That's probably not going to work for me."

She sat up. "Why not? Don't tell me you have to work tonight."

"There's rain in the forecast for Monday. I want to finish planting that short-season corn on the south forty."

"I thought you were going to finish planting that this morning."

"The tractor broke down, and it took me most of the morning to fix it. I was almost late for Sam's graduation."

Disappointment dampened her mood. She knew it wasn't Pete's fault that the tractor had broken down, but it was his fault that he was so stubborn. If he'd just ask his dad for help once in a while maybe he wouldn't be so far behind and they could go out tonight.

"You're mad," he said, glancing over at her.

"I'm not mad. I'm just . . . frustrated."

Pete turned onto the gravel road. "This is what life is like when you're married to a farmer. You know that."

"It doesn't have to be this bad," Dana said. "You could apologize to your dad and ask him to help you."

Pete shook his head. "I wouldn't have to replant the south forty if it wasn't for his mistake. He certainly hasn't apologized to me for it, but I'm trying not to hold it against him."

Dana wasn't sure what to say. They'd been through this

before. "Just think about letting this go, Pete, for the sake of your family. You know how much your dad loves the farm. Invite him to be part of it again."

Pete didn't say anything for the rest of the trip, but she hoped he was taking her words to heart. If he just gave a little, she thought Bob would meet him the rest of the way. She just hoped he did it before the rift got too wide and deep between them.

Pete pulled into the farm, where several cars lined the driveway. "It looks like there are quite a few people here already."

As they got out of the car, Dana saw Bill standing in the backyard watching Jennifer and Madison play with Toby. He turned as Dana and Pete approached the back door.

"I need to talk to you," Bill told his brother.

"Well, hello to you too," Pete said. "What do you want to talk about?"

Before Bill could reply, Jennifer and Madison ran up to him.

"Daddy, can we go inside and have cake now?" Madison asked him.

"Please, Daddy," Jennifer pleaded. "I ate all of my sandwich."

Bill gave a short nod. "Go on in and tell your mom I said you could have some cake. Be sure and wash your hands before you eat."

"We will," Jennifer promised as the two girls ran to the door.

Dana was about to follow them when Bill said something that stopped her in her tracks.

"What's wrong with you, Pete? Why won't you take part in the reenactment? You know how much it means to Dad."

Dana closed her eyes, knowing Bill's tone wouldn't go over well with her husband.

"I have responsibilities, you know," Pete replied. "I'm not a hotshot lawyer like you. I can't take time out to play war games."

"You can't take one day off?" Bill asked incredulously. "It's a national holiday."

"Farmers don't get holidays or weekends off. You know that."

Bill shook his head, obviously not satisfied with the answer. Dana wished he would let it go, but she was too new to the family to feel as if she could intervene.

"You're just being stubborn," Bill said. "You know Dad doesn't ask much of us, and the one time he does ask, you turn him down."

"You seem a lot more upset about the whole thing than he is," Pete replied. "Or did he send you out here to hound me about it?"

Bill snorted. "You know Dad better than that."

Dana could feel an argument brewing and tried to think of a way to stop it. She could tell by the muscle flexing in Pete's jaw that he was getting angry. He didn't like people telling him what to do—especially his older brother.

But Bill either didn't realize the effect his words were having on Pete or he didn't care.

"You need to find yourself a uniform," Bill told him, "and join the rest of us in this reenactment. I don't think that's too much to ask, considering everything Dad's done for you."

Pete's eyes narrowed. "What's that supposed to mean?"

"I mean you practically lived with Mom and Dad until

you got married. I know you're running the farm now, but you ate plenty of meals with them and counted on both of them whenever you needed help. I just think it's payback time."

Dana knew any progress she'd made with Pete concerning his father had just gone down the drain. "Why don't we go in now?" she said to Pete, hoping to avoid further damage.

"That's a good idea." Pete turned and followed Dana to the back door.

"Think about what I said," Bill called after him.

Dana had no doubt that Pete would do just that. Bill had his heart in the right place, but he obviously didn't know his brother very well. Now Dana was back to square one and wasn't sure what to do next.

Chapter Twenty-Three

The house was brimming with people as Charlotte refilled the big bowl of pasta salad on the kitchen table. She'd moved all the chairs into the living room to allow for easier movement around the table as the guests filled their plates. She'd placed the sandwiches and salads at one end and Hannah's beautiful cake at the other.

"Emily," Charlotte called out, spying her granddaughter in the hallway talking to Troy, "will you take a picture of this cake for me before we cut it?"

"Sure, Grandma," Emily said, pulling her pink digital camera out of her pocket.

Hannah walked up beside Charlotte, a pitcher of ice water in her hands. "I'm glad you like the cake."

"I love it," Charlotte said, admiring the way it was neatly decorated with green frosting on top to look like a soccer field. There was even a little figure dressed as a soccer player kicking a ball into the goal. The writing on the cake read, "Happy Graduation, Sam! You're a winner!"

"It's much better than a cake with just flowers on it," Emily said after snapping the picture. "This one really means something to Sam."

Then she turned around and motioned for Hannah and Charlotte to move closer together. "Now it's your turn," Emily said. "Smile."

"Hold on," Hannah said, setting down the pitcher of water and then circling her arm around Charlotte's waist. "Okay, I'm ready now."

Charlotte leaned in close to Hannah, grateful for all her help and support. She thanked God once again for having such a special friend in her life.

"Okay," Hannah said, picking up the pitcher once more. "Now I'd better go refill some water glasses."

After she'd disappeared down the hallway, Charlotte turned to Emily. "I'd like you to do me a favor."

"Sure, Grandma, what is it?"

"I want you to spend the next fifteen minutes or so taking candid shots of Sam and his guests and then print off all the pictures for me, including the ones you took at graduation. Can you do that for me?"

Emily looked surprised by the request. "I can do it, but do you need them right away?"

"The sooner, the better," Charlotte told her as more guests found their way into the kitchen. She was pleased to see Pastor Evans and his wife, Nancy.

"Welcome," Charlotte said, walking up to greet them. "I'm so glad you could make it."

"We're happy to be here," Pastor Evans said, taking her hand, "and so proud of Sam. That young man's traveled a long, hard journey to get to this point."

His words touched Charlotte. Sometimes she got so caught up in the drama of day-to-day living that she forgot to step back and look at the big picture. Sam had come a long way since arriving in Bedford two years ago. That grief-stricken, rebellious teenage boy was turning into a fine young man, give or take a few stumbles here and there.

"What a lovely spread," Nancy said, looking over at the kitchen table.

"Please help yourselves," Charlotte told them. "There are paper plates and napkins on the table, along with some plastic utensils. If you need anything, just let me know."

"I'm sure we'll be just fine," Nancy assured her. "I like the way you've decorated the house."

"Did Nicole come with you?" Charlotte asked, looking around for their daughter.

"I'm afraid she had another graduation reception to attend," Nancy said as the pastor moved toward the table.

Charlotte thanked God for small favors. The farther apart Emily and Nicole stayed, the better.

Dana walked up to her with a smile of apology. "I'm sorry it took me so long to get here. Please tell me what I can do to help."

"I think I've got everything under control," Charlotte said, watching Pete join in the food line behind Pastor Evans and Nancy. "I'm just keeping an eye on the sandwiches and salad so they don't run out."

"Let me do that," Dana insisted. "You go out and visit with your guests."

"Are you sure?" Charlotte asked, tempted by the offer. She'd put Christopher in charge of opening the front door and receiving gifts while Bob played host in the living room. Sam was in there too, and she wanted to see how he was enjoying the party.

"I'm absolutely sure," Dana said, nudging her toward

the hallway. "I'll take care of everything in here. You go out there and have a good time."

Charlotte didn't argue with her. As she headed for the living room, she was happy to see Melody and her family walking through the front door. Melody handed a card to Christopher, who placed it in the card basket on the end table.

"I'm so glad you could come," Charlotte greeted them.

"We wouldn't miss it," Melody said. "Wow, there are a lot of people here."

Charlotte turned to look at all their guests, pleased to see that almost everyone they'd invited had shown up. *Except Kevin.* Sam hadn't said anything about his father's absence, and she didn't intend to bring it up. As far as Kevin was concerned, "out of sight, out of mind" was her motto for the rest of the day.

"How are you, Russ?" she asked Melody's husband. Ashley and Brett Givens stood behind their parents.

"Just fine," Russ replied.

"Well, I've got plenty of food in the kitchen," she told them. "So please help yourselves."

Russ turned to his son. "Are you hungry?"

Melody laughed. "I think we all know the answer to that question."

Brett grinned. "I'm starved. I haven't eaten for at least an hour."

Russ and the kids moved toward the kitchen while Melody watched them go with an amused sigh. "I'm not sure Brett will ever stop eating. And it's probably a good thing, since he's still a beanpole. I don't know where he puts all that food."

"He's a growing boy," Charlotte said. "Sam's finally

slowed down his eating a bit, but Christopher is starting to resemble a bottomless pit."

More guests arrived—high school friends of Sam—so Charlotte and Melody moved away from the door.

"I don't want to monopolize the hostess," Melody told her. "Can I help you with anything?"

"Thanks, but I think I have everything covered."

"Then I'm going to grab a plate of food. I hope there's still some left after Brett fills his plate."

Charlotte chuckled as Melody headed for the kitchen; she mingled with the other guests. Sam stood near the window, the center of attention. He seemed to be enjoying himself, and Charlotte appreciated the way he greeted each guest. She saw Bill and Anna visiting with Frank Carter in the corner of the room, the baby asleep in Anna's arms. She'd barely had a chance to visit with them since they arrived, and she hoped they'd stay for a while after the reception was over.

Charlotte visited with some of the guests and then waited until Sam had a rare moment alone to walk up to him. "How are you doing?"

"Great," he said. "I can't believe all these people are here because of me."

"They're here because they care about you."

Emily brought Bob over to them. "Okay, you three, let's take a picture."

Sam stood between Charlotte and Bob as Emily snapped the picture. She looked at the screen and smiled her approval. "Very nice."

"My mouth is starting to hurt from smiling," Sam said, reaching up to rub his jaw.

"The reception will last only another two hours or so," Charlotte told him. "Then you can relax and enjoy the rest of the day."

"I can't wait to get out of these clothes," Sam said, referring to the shirt and tie he wore, along with a pair of khaki slacks. She'd tried to talk him into wearing a suit for graduation, but he'd flatly refused.

"You and me both, kid," Bob said, straightening his tie.

Emily rolled her eyes. "Men. I love getting dressed up."

"I want to take a picture of you three kids together," Charlotte said, waving Christopher over to them.

Emily handed her the camera and then stood between her two brothers. They posed together while Charlotte snapped the picture.

"Hold on," Charlotte said after looking at the screen. "I need to take another picture. Christopher has his eyes closed in this one."

"Way to go, Christopher," Sam teased.

Charlotte snapped another photograph. "There. That one's perfect."

She handed Emily the camera. "Be sure and get one of Bill and his family, as well as Pete and Dana."

"I'm on it, Grandma." Emily walked over to Troy and whispered something in his ear; they both laughed.

Charlotte spent the next hour talking with guests and thanking others as they departed. She talked with Sam's boss, Ed Haffner, as well as the church youth group leader, Jason Vink, who was grateful for Sam's help on the recent Shelter for Nebraska volunteer project.

By the time five o'clock rolled around, Charlotte's feet were starting to ache in her navy blue heels.

She looked around the house for Emily, wondering if she'd printed out those pictures yet. Charlotte wanted them for a special project she intended to work on as soon as the last guest left.

"Have you seen your sister?" she asked Christopher after she'd checked the family room and kitchen.

"I think she went upstairs with Troy."

Charlotte looked toward the stairs, hoping Christopher was mistaken. Emily knew she wasn't allowed to have boys in her room. As she headed for the stairs, Bill and Anna intercepted her.

"We're going to take off now, Mom," Bill told her.

"I was hoping you could stay and visit for a while after the reception was over."

"Sorry," Anna said. "The kids are exhausted. We'll have to do it another time."

Charlotte nodded and then reached out to take Will from Bill's arms. She snuggled the baby for a few moments and then kissed the top of his head. "You'll be here on Memorial Day, right?"

"I wouldn't miss it," Bill told her, giving Charlotte a hug. She walked them all to the front door.

"Bye, Grandma," Madison said, with Jennifer echoing a good-bye of her own.

Charlotte leaned down to kiss and hug her little granddaughters. "Bye, girls. Thanks for coming today. I'll see you again soon."

After they left, Charlotte continued on her mission to find Emily. Sam sat on the living room sofa talking to Pete, Dana, and Grandma Maxie while Bob chatted with Frank Carter. She passed by them and headed up the stairs.

She could hear voices coming from Emily's room, but the door was closed. Charlotte walked over to the bedroom door and leaned her head close but couldn't make out anything. Without knocking, she opened the door.

Emily and Troy flew apart as Charlotte entered the room. They were standing in the middle of the bedroom and both had guilty expressions on their faces.

"What's going on here?" Charlotte asked.

"It's not what you think, Grandma." Emily said quickly.

Charlotte sincerely hoped that was true. "You know that boys aren't allowed up here alone with you, Emily. There's no excuse for this."

"We're not alone," Emily protested, pointing behind Charlotte. "See?"

Charlotte turned around to look through the open doorway and saw Ashley emerging from the bathroom.

"Ashley's been up here with us the whole time. I swear she was only gone for like two seconds."

Ashley walked into the bedroom. "What's going on?"

"That's what I came up here to find out," Charlotte said, wondering if she was overreacting. In any event, she didn't want to cause a scene while they still had guests in the house.

"Have you printed those pictures for me yet, Emily?"

"Not yet." Emily grabbed her camera. "I'll do it right now. Come on, you guys."

Charlotte watched Troy and Ashley follow Emily down the stairs. She still didn't know what had happened, but there was no doubt that she'd startled Emily and Troy when she'd entered that room.

She walked back downstairs, telling herself she'd deal with it later. Emily had been so good lately. Charlotte didn't want to think her granddaughter had been fooling her this whole time.

"What's going on?" Bob asked her when she reached the living room.

"Nothing," she told him, moving toward the door to say good-bye to Frank and Hannah.

"Thank you so much for all your help." She gave Hannah a big hug.

"It was my pleasure," Hannah replied. "Everyone seemed to like the cake I made for Sam. Believe it or not, I even got a few cake orders."

Charlotte smiled. "I believe it."

After the other guests started to leave, Charlotte headed for the family room where Emily sat at the computer.

"Here are the pictures, Grandma," Emily said, handing them to her. "What do you need them for?"

"You'll see," Charlotte promised. "Where are Troy and Ashley?"

"They left out the back door." Emily turned off the computer. "I hope you're not mad at Troy, Grandma. Or at me. We really didn't do anything wrong."

Emily sounded sincere and Charlotte wanted to believe her, but it had been only a week since Emily had tried to sneak out for the late-night party. Still, she didn't want anything to mar Sam's day, so she decided to give Emily another chance.

"I'll let it go this time," Charlotte told her. "But I don't want it to happen again."

"It won't," Emily said solemnly. "I promise."

Charlotte believed her. "Okay, why don't you go start cleaning up the kitchen for me? I'll be there to help you in a little bit."

"Okay," she said without complaint.

Charlotte took the pictures into her bedroom and then added them to the gift she'd made for Sam. She kicked off her heels, replacing them with a pair of slippers.

"That feels much better," she murmured to herself, enjoying the few moments of peace in her bedroom. She walked over to the window and looked outside. The cars were gone. The party had been a success.

"Thank you, Lord," Charlotte prayed, "for bringing Sam to this special moment in his life. Guide him the rest of the way and let him know Your unconditional love for him. Please watch over him, Lord, now and always. Amen."

She wiped a tear from her eye and then gathered herself for a moment before she walked out of the bedroom. When she reached the kitchen she saw the family, including Pete and Dana, gathered around the table. It had been cleared of food and cake and was now stacked with gifts.

"Look at all these presents," Sam said, his eyes wide. "I never expected so much."

"It's a big day for you," Charlotte said. "Gifts are one way of recognizing your achievement."

"Look what Uncle Bill and Aunt Anna gave me." Sam reached down and picked up a large piece of luggage with a big red bow on it. "There are more suitcases inside this one. It's a whole set!"

"You can take a picture of them with the camera we gave you," Pete joked.

"I love the camera too, Uncle Pete," Sam said. "It's awesome. I must have taken about a hundred pictures with it already today."

"Open the rest of your presents, Sam," Christopher prodded. "I want to see what else you got."

Dana grabbed a notepad to record the gifts received and who had given each one. Charlotte knew that would come in handy when it was time to prod Sam to write thank-you notes.

As Charlotte watched Sam ooh and ahh over his gifts, she started to wonder if he'd be disappointed with the one from her and Bob. She'd put a lot of thought into it, but it wasn't as exciting as a digital camera or a set of luggage. She hadn't even brought it out to the table yet, wanting to wait until the right moment.

When he finished opening the gifts, Sam turned to the basket of cards on the table.

"I'm glad I can finally begin to open these," Sam said, referring to the few that had come in the mail earlier that week. The rest had been brought by reception guests, and they contained varying amounts of cash along with several gift cards.

"Wow," Christopher said, as Sam pulled another twenty out of a card. "You're going to be rich!"

"You should put some of that in a savings account," Bob advised. "Save it for a rainy day."

"I will," Sam replied, reaching for the last card. He opened it, and a fifty-dollar bill fluttered onto the table.

Pete whistled low. "Wow, someone was generous. Who is that one from?"

Sam slowly looked up from the card. "It's from my dad."

Charlotte could tell Sam was as shocked as the rest of the family. There was no return address on the envelope, but there was a postage mark from somewhere in Texas. She assumed it had arrived in the mail sometime during the past week with some of the other cards.

"Did he write anything on it?" Emily asked.

Sam cleared his throat. "Dear Sam, I'm sorry I couldn't make it to your graduation today. I hope you have a good time and that we can get together soon. Love, Dad."

"That's it?" Pete asked.

"Yeah." Sam set the card on the table. "I really didn't expect him to come anyway."

She could hear the disappointment in his voice as the rest of the family fell silent. Charlotte didn't want Sam's big day to end on this note, so she thought now was the perfect time to give Sam his gift from her and Bob.

"You still have one more present to open," Charlotte told him.

"I do?"

"Hold on." Charlotte moved toward the hallway. "I'll get it."

A minute later, she returned with a blue gift bag topped with white tissue paper. "Here you go. This is from Grandpa and me."

Sam took the bag from her and opened it, pulling out a photo album. "Wow," he said, sounding less than enthused. "Thanks, Grandma."

"Open it," she urged him.

Sam opened the cover, his eyes widening when he saw a picture of himself as a baby. "What is this?"

"It's your journey though life up to this point," Charlotte told him.

Sam slowly paged through the pictures, laughing at some of the photos showing him as a young child and smiling at the one with Denise giving him a big hug.

Charlotte had carefully arranged the photos of Sam's life from his birth to his graduation.

"That's why you wanted those pictures," Emily said, when Sam reached the final pages of the book. "I wondered why you were in such a hurry."

On the very last page was an inscription and an envelope. The inscription read, "Wherever you go in life, you'll always have a home with us." Sam reached for the envelope and opened it, taking out a hundred-dollar bill. "Wow," he said. "I've never held one of these before. Thanks."

"You're welcome," Charlotte told him. "Grandpa and I are very proud of you."

Sam walked over to her and gave her a big hug. "I love the scrapbook, Grandma, and I love you. Thanks for everything."

Tears of happiness filled her eyes. Sam wasn't one to throw the phrase *I love you* around very much, so she knew that when he said it, he really meant. "I love you too, Sam."

Sam gave his grandpa a hug next as Bob patted him on the back.

"Put that money somewhere safe until you can get it in the bank," Bob told him as Sam pulled away.

Sam laughed. "I will, Grandpa."

"Well, I hate to break up this tender moment," Pete said, a twinkle in his eyes. "But I think I'm ready for more cake. I only had three pieces."

Everyone laughed and then began to drift off to other parts of the house while Charlotte cut a piece of cake for Pete. She wrapped up another piece for Dana to take home.

She couldn't have asked for a better day or for better grandchildren. "Thank you, God," she prayed, joy filling her heart, "for everything."

Chapter Twenty-Four

By Monday after school, Christopher had finally worked up enough courage to confess the truth to George Kimball.

The guilt over burning the victory rosebush had made Christopher feel sick for the last few days. He knew George would probably be mad at him, maybe even hate him, but he couldn't let himself chicken out. That's not what a good soldier would do. After reading Great-Grandpa Les's letters and listening to George's stories about the war, Christopher thought he understood what it meant to be a good soldier. It was about honor and duty and doing the right thing even if you were afraid.

And, at this moment, Christopher was terrified.

He stood in front of Uncle George's house on Locust Street, trying to figure out exactly what he was going to say. When nothing came to him, he walked up to the porch, knowing that at the very least, he could say he was sorry.

Christopher knocked on the door, lightly at first and then a little harder. The sooner he got this over with, the better.

A few moments later, the door opened and Uncle George stood with his cane on the other side.

"Christopher! What a nice surprise." Uncle George said with a smile. "Good thing I bought some more butterscotch candy yesterday. Come on in, son."

But Christopher stood his ground, certain Uncle George wouldn't want him in his house when he found out who had burned his rosebush. "I've got to tell you something."

Uncle George looked concerned. "Is something wrong?" he asked, stepping out onto the porch.

Christopher took a deep breath and then made his confession. "I'm the one who burned your rosebush."

Uncle George's eyes widened in surprise. "That was you?"

Christopher nodded. "Me and . . ." He caught himself just in time before saying Dylan's name. He didn't want to drag his friend into it, especially since Christopher was the one who had actually shot the second rocket that day.

"I didn't mean to do it," Christopher continued, watching Uncle George closely for his reaction. "I was shooting off a couple of really old fireworks in the empty lot behind your house. They were supposed to go straight up into the air and then explode into confetti."

Uncle George's eyes narrowed. "Did your grandmother give you permission to shoot those fireworks?"

Christopher lowered his head. "No sir, but I did it anyway. The second rocket took off toward your yard before we could stop it and landed in your victory rosebush. I'm awfully sorry."

Uncle George didn't say anything for several moments,

making Christopher even more nervous. He wasn't sure if he should turn around and leave or wait for Uncle George to yell at him.

But Uncle George didn't yell at him. He leaned heavily on his cane and looked Christopher in the eye. "I was pretty mad that day."

"I know," Christopher said. "That's why we ran away."

"You and the Lonetree boy?" Uncle George asked.

Christopher blinked in surprise. "You know Dylan?"

"I've seen him around the neighborhood and asked some of the other kids about him. He has some sort of . . . physical problem, doesn't he?"

"Yes," Christopher replied, "but he gets along all right. Some of the kids at school make fun of him though."

Uncle George nodded. "I used to stutter when I was a child, so some of the kids made fun of me too."

He was amazed by the fact that Uncle George didn't seem mad, especially now that Christopher knew how much that rosebush meant to him.

"So," Uncle George continued, "what are we going to do now?"

"What do you mean?"

"You came here like a man to tell me what you did wrong. Now tell me how you're going to make it right."

Christopher gulped, not certain what to tell him. He dug into his pocket and found two quarters. "Here's fifty cents." He held the quarters out to Uncle George. "I can pay you every week until you can afford a new rosebush."

"You can keep your money," Uncle George told him. "That victory rosebush out back isn't dead—it's just wounded. It needs some tender loving care to help it come back and bloom again."

Christopher slipped the quarters back into his pocket. "Do you want me to come and help you take care of it?"

"That would be a good start," Uncle George told him. "Maybe you could do some work around the yard for me this summer too. I don't get around as well as I'd like, and this is a big yard."

"I can do that," Christopher agreed, feeling a little better already. "I know how to mow and rake leaves and stuff."

"That's just what I need," Uncle George said. "And you can invite your friend Dylan along too, if he'd like to come. But be sure and tell him I don't bite."

"Oh, he doesn't think you bite," Christopher said, taking him seriously. "He was afraid you might hit us with your cane."

Uncle George shook his head. "I would never hit anybody. My days of combat ended when I came home from the war. My Helen was at the train station to welcome me, wearing a yellow rose corsage from that victory rosebush." He looked off into the distance. "Now I take yellow roses to her grave, knowing that someday she'll welcome me to our heavenly home."

Christopher didn't say anything, sensing that Uncle George was far away.

At last Uncle George cleared his throat and then looked down at him. "I'm proud of you, Christopher, for standing up like a man and telling me what you'd done."

Christopher didn't feel like he deserved the praise. "But I didn't tell you right when it happened. I ran away instead."

"Well, it takes practice to be a man. How old are you? Eleven? Twelve?"

"I turned twelve in March."

Uncle George nodded. "Then I'd say you've got a good start on the road to manhood. It's not always easy to face up to what you've done, but it sure beats being afraid."

As the words sank in, Christopher realized he was right. He'd spent so much time being afraid of Old Man Kimball he'd even risked getting in trouble at school instead of just doing the right thing.

"Now why don't you come inside for a bit," Uncle George said. "We can figure out what chores you can do for me this summer. You can also help me eat some of that butterscotch candy. I'll make sure and put that on the list."

Christopher followed Uncle George into the house, remembering how frightened he'd been of Old Man Kimball just a couple of weeks ago. Now Christopher considered him one of his friends.

ON TUESDAY MORNING, Bob drained the last of his coffee and made an announcement. "I'm going to try on Dad's old uniform today. It's time I find out if it's going to fit me or not."

Charlotte stood at the kitchen sink, washing breakfast dishes. Emily and Christopher had left for school awhile ago, and Sam had gone into town to talk to Ed Haffner about increasing his hours at the airport now that he was out of school.

"Okay," Charlotte told him, hoping he'd lost enough weight to wear Les's uniform.

A few minutes, later Bob emerged from the bedroom. "It doesn't fit."

She turned around to see him wearing the uniform, the shirt hanging out over the pants. He'd been able to easily close more buttons on the shirt, but the last few buttons still gaped.

"Maybe you can tuck that part into the pants," she suggested.

"That might work if I could get the pants closed, but that's not going to happen anytime soon. I guess I was fatter than I thought."

She could hear the disappointment in his voice and walked over to evaluate the fit. If it was close, she might be able to let out a few seams.

"I'm sorry, Bob," she said at last. "I don't think there's any way we can make this work."

"I know," he said. "I should have figured that out the first time I tried it on."

She looked up at him. "You did lose a nice amount of weight though. That counts for something."

"Not for what matters," he said, heading back into the bedroom to change.

She stared after him, wishing she knew a way to make him feel better. He'd wanted to wear that uniform so badly. It gave him a connection to his father, and now it would have to stay in the closet. Even the grandsons couldn't wear it. The uniform was too short for Sam and too big for Christopher.

Bob walked into the kitchen once more, dressed in his blue jeans and a short-sleeved shirt. "I guess I should have thought of a backup plan. I was just so sure that uniform would fit me."

Charlotte cleared her throat. "I thought of a backup plan for you. Rosemary agreed to make you a uniform in case Les's didn't fit."

Bob nodded. "Well, good thing somebody around here is thinking ahead. It wouldn't look too good if the organizer of the war reenactment wasn't taking part in it."

"I'll go into Fabrics and Fun today to see if she's done with it," Charlotte told him. "I ordered some for the boys too, so I can pick those up at the same time."

He sat down at the kitchen table. "Take your time. I'm not going anywhere."

Charlotte wanted to suggest that he go out and help Pete, but she figured now probably wasn't the best time. She could tell he was still upset about the uniform and probably just needed some time alone.

"Okay," she told him. "I'll leave as soon as I finish these dishes."

A half hour later, Charlotte walked into Fabrics and Fun. Rosemary was waiting on another customer, so Charlotte bided her time by looking over the quilting supplies. She'd been thinking about making a wedding-ring quilt to give Dana and Pete as a housewarming gift when they moved into their new house. If she decided to do it, she'd need to get started on it soon.

"Hello, Charlotte," Rosemary greeted her as the other customer headed toward the door. "I'm glad you stopped by today. I finished Bob's uniform last night, and I want to get your opinion on it."

"Talk about perfect timing," Charlotte said. "That's why I'm here. Bob tried on Les's uniform this morning, and it's not going to fit him in time for the war reenactment."

"Oh, that's too bad," Rosemary exclaimed. "Was he disappointed?"

"I'm afraid so, but he did seem to feel a little better when he heard that you were making him a uniform."

Rosemary smiled. "Then our covert mission was a success. Let me go in the back and get it."

A moment later, she was back with a khaki uniform. "I tried to distress the fabric a little bit," Rosemary said, "to give it an authentic vintage look. What do you think?"

Charlotte looked at the uniform in amazement, her spirits lifting. "I think no one will be able to tell the difference. This is wonderful, Rosemary."

She blushed. "Thank you. I enjoyed doing it. I hope Bob likes it."

"I'm sure he will." Charlotte took the uniform from her. "And I'd like to pay you something for it. You went to a lot of work here."

Rosemary held up both hands. "No payment necessary. You took on the USO dance for me. Believe me, that's payment enough. How's it going, by the way?"

"Pretty well, I think," Charlotte replied. "Of course, it always scares me if I feel too comfortable about an event I've planned; that usually means I'm forgetting something."

Rosemary chuckled. "Isn't that always the way? I'm sure everything will work out just fine."

"Will you be coming?"

Rosemary hesitated. "Oh, I don't know. I won't have Jerome there to dance with me, so..."

"You know Bob doesn't like to dance either," Charlotte told her. "We can dance together if we can't find other partners."

She could see Rosemary was starting to waver. "Come on. It will be fun. We're serving food made from recipes concocted during the war, so you have to be there to try some of the dishes."

Rosemary smiled. "All right, I surrender. I'll come to the dance. I should probably be there anyway since I'm on the events committee."

"Good." Charlotte tucked the uniform under one arm. "Are the uniforms I ordered for Sam and Christopher in yet?"

"Not yet," Rosemary told her. "I talked to the company this morning, and they promised to have them here by Friday. They're usually pretty reliable, so I wouldn't worry about it."

"I won't," Charlotte said, trusting Rosemary's judgment. "Maybe I'll drive in Saturday afternoon to pick them up."

"Don't even think about it. You're going to be too busy getting ready for the USO dance that night. I'll bring the uniforms with me to the dance, and you can take them home with you."

"Sounds good," Charlotte replied. "Did I tell you we're going to have a jitterbug contest?" As soon as she asked the question, Charlotte remembered something she'd forgotten to do.

"Oh, no!"

"What is it?" Rosemary asked.

"I just realized I forgot to ask Anita Wilson to help judge the jitterbug contest." Charlotte headed for the door. "I'd better go do it right now. I'll see you Saturday, Rosemary. Thanks again for making Bob's uniform."

"Bye, Charlotte."

She hurried to her car and drove straight to Anita's house. Charlotte couldn't believe she'd let that slip her mind. She wasn't even certain Anita was planning to attend the USO dance, although she certainly hoped so.

When she pulled into the driveway, she saw Anita in the front yard watering her peony bushes. Charlotte turned off the engine and then climbed out of her car.

"This is a nice surprise," Anita said as she shut off the hose.

Charlotte walked over to her. "I'm here to ask you a favor, Anita. And I really hope you'll say yes."

Curiosity lit her blue eyes. "What kind of favor?'

"I'm planning to hold a jitterbug contest during the USO dance on Saturday night. Lydia Middleton has already agreed to be one of the judges, and I was hoping you'd be one as well."

Anita smiled. "Now that sounds like my kind of fun. Even if I can't jitterbug anymore, I can tell others the right way to do it."

"Is that a yes?" Charlotte asked hopefully.

"You bet it is."

Charlotte reached out to hug her. "Oh, I'm so happy. I can't wait for Saturday night. I just hope I've done everything right."

"Do you want me to come and look the place over for you?"

"Would you? That would be wonderful."

"Then I'll plan on it. But I'm sure you've got everything under control. Opal always said you were smart as a whip."

Charlotte laughed. "Well, as my mother, she might have been a little biased."

"If you can't brag about your own kids to your best friend, who can you brag to?"

"Good point," Charlotte replied, remembering all the times she'd shared her grandkids' achievements with Hannah. "So I'll see you on Saturday night?"

"You sure will." Anita smiled. "Be there or be square."

Chapter Twenty-Five

On Thursday evening, Dana and Pete walked around inside the shell of their new house looking at the framed walls that had been erected but not yet covered with drywall.

"This is so weird," Dana said, standing in the spot that would someday be her kitchen. "We can actually see what the rooms are going to look like now."

"The builders still have a long way to go," Pete said, checking the strength of one of the beams. "But at least it's actually starting to look like a real house now."

Dana walked around, trying to picture how each room would look with the walls painted and the furniture in place. She planned to use much of her summer to research decorating ideas. She wanted to try some different painting techniques on the walls and color coordinate the master bathroom with a beautiful wallpaper border she'd found on clearance in Harding.

"I wish the builders would do a little better job of cleaning up when they're done for the day." Pete leaned down to pick up an empty Styrofoam cup. "They seem to be getting a lot worse lately."

She stared at her husband. "Didn't you know that your dad used to clean up after them?"

He tossed the cup into a trash can. "What are you talking about?"

"I came here one Saturday to talk to the electrician about light fixtures. I think you were out planting corn or something." Dana brushed a strand of hair out of her eyes. "The builders had already left, and your dad was here picking up after them."

"No," Pete said quietly. "I didn't know that."

"I think there are a lot of cleanup jobs he does around the farm to save you time."

Pete held up his hands. "We're not going to have this discussion again, are we, Dana? Haven't we talked about it enough?"

"Obviously not, because the problem between you two still isn't solved."

She moved closer to him, seeing the frustration in his eyes. The last thing she wanted was to fight with her husband, but this had gone on long enough. If he would just listen to her, really listen, then maybe she could finally get through to him. It had almost worked the day of Sam's graduation, until Bill had started pulling his big-brother act.

"There is no problem," Pete told her. "We get along just fine."

"On the surface," she agreed. "But it's not the same as it was before, and you know it. What I can't understand is why you're letting it go on for so long."

"Don't you get it?" Pete walked over to their future living room and looked out the new picture window that had just recently been put in. It provided a perfect view of Heather Creek.

"I was always the screwup in the family," Pete continued. "Bill was the golden child, Denise was the rebel, and I was the screwup."

Dana winced at his sharp tone but didn't take it personally. Maybe if he got whatever was really bothering him off his chest, they could finally get past this.

"That was how you saw yourself a long time ago," she said gently. "Nobody thinks you're a screwup now. Especially not me."

Pete shook his head. "That's not the way I see it. Dad was all too ready to blame the ruined soybean field on me. He called it dumb. He might as well have called *me* dumb, because that's what he meant."

Dana was learning that despite Pete's wisecracking personality, he was really a very sensitive soul. Bob and Pete had both hurt each other, and neither seemed to know how to heal their wounds.

She walked over to him and lightly placed her hand on his arm. "You're all grown up now, Pete. You have to let the past go. Nobody in this family thinks you're dumb. You're running a farm that supports two families. That's not something just anybody could do."

"But you still think I need Dad's help," Pete said bitterly.

That's when she realized her mistake. She'd been urging him to take Bob back so he could help him around the farm. Pete had seen that as a lack of confidence in him. That's why he'd been resisting her and Charlotte's attempts to get things back to the way they used to be.

"I think you both need each other," she said carefully.

"Not because you can't handle the job alone, but because you're family."

He didn't say anything, his gaze fixed on the window.

"You know, Pete," she continued, "at the wedding I realized that my dad is getting older. I mean, he's in good health, but the reality hit me that I don't know how long I'll be blessed to have him in my life."

Pete turned to look at her. "You're worried about him?"

"Not worried, exactly. Just aware that he's getting older and none of us knows what the future holds." She looked into Pete's eyes. "I'd give anything to see my dad every day like you get to see yours. The chance to work together with him would just be icing on the cake."

Pete reached for her hand. "As soon as planting season is over, we can start going to Grand Island more often."

"I'd like that," she said. "And I'd also like you to think about welcoming your dad back into your life on the farm. Not because you need him, but because the day is going to come when he won't be here anymore."

He sighed. "I know you're right. It's just . . . hard for me."

She squeezed his hand. "Just promise me you'll think about it.

He leaned in to kiss her. "I promise."

Chapter Twenty-Six

Charlotte stood at the back door of the high school gym on Saturday evening, waiting for the van carrying the band to park. The alumni banquet had just ended, and now some of the men, including Bob, Sam, and Christopher, were taking the tables down so that the dance could begin. She was hoping Pete and Dana would come, but she hadn't seen them yet.

A man got out of the driver's seat. His hair was cut short, and he wore a suit that could have come straight out of the 1940s. "Mrs. Stevenson?"

"Yes, I'm Charlotte Stevenson." She reached out to shake his hand. "Are you Mr. Booker?"

"That's right," said the band leader. "You can call me Clive."

"I was afraid you weren't going to make it on time."

"Sorry about that," Clive said. "We had a flat tire on our way from Kearney." He looked inside the gym. "Where do you want us to set up?"

"Over by the basketball hoop," she told him. "There should be plenty of outlets. Let me know if you need anything else, and I'll do my best to accommodate you."

"Will do," Clive replied. "We'll be ready to go in about twenty minutes."

Charlotte checked her watch. "That should be just about right."

She left him to go check on the food tables. Emily was in charge of unwrapping all the containers of food and setting them on the table. Rosemary had pitched in to help her, and now they were placing serving utensils in the dishes that needed them.

"This food looks wonderful," Charlotte said, amazed at the variety before her. There were all kinds of dishes, some she recognized and many she didn't.

"It tastes wonderful too," Rosemary told her. "I sampled a few of them in the kitchen. Just a few nibbles, mind you."

Charlotte smiled. "I'm a nibbler myself, so I know exactly what you mean."

She'd brought three cherry-berry pies and three caramel-apple pies. It had been difficult to adjust the recipes to fit the war rationing of the forties, but she'd made it work. Instead of sugar, Charlotte had used a mixture of applesauce and corn syrup to sweeten the pies. Just to be on the safe side, she'd baked a practice pie first, and it tasted fine. They might not be as good as the original recipe, but none of the kids had complained.

Many of the guests from the alumni banquet had gone on a tour of the school after the banquet was over, but they were starting to amble back inside. Most of the tables had been cleared, with a few set up around the perimeter of the gym along with extra chairs. The tables framed a perfect dance floor, and Charlotte hoped people would take advantage of it. That was her main fear—that no one would dance.

As the band started warming up, more people entered the gym. To Charlotte's delight, it looked to her like there was going to be a big crowd. When someone called her name, she quickly turned around, loving the way the skirt of her vintage dress swirled around her.

"There you are," Anita said, walking over to her. "I'm sorry I'm late. My grandson called me from his ship, and I just couldn't cut the call short."

Charlotte knew Anita's grandson was serving in the navy and currently was stationed on a ship in the Atlantic. "I don't blame you a bit. I would have done the same thing." She looked around the gym. "Everything seems to be going smoothly so far. Do you see anything missing?"

Anita turned in a slow circle, taking in everything. "It's amazing, Charlotte. I feel like you've taken me back eighty years. There's music and food and men in uniform. It makes me feel all giddy inside."

She'd talked Bob and the boys into putting their uniforms on when they got there and was happy to see that other men taking part in the reenactment were wearing their uniforms as well. Many of the woman had dressed the part too and had done their hair and makeup in the forties style. Charlotte's own hair had been too short to put into a forties-style bob, but Emily had helped her style it so she'd fit in with everyone else.

Charlotte looked at her watch. "It looks like it's almost time to start." She took a deep breath. "I need to go up on stage and welcome everyone. Wish me luck."

"I'll be rooting for you," Anita said. "If you need me, I'll be over at the food table sampling some of Janet Corcoran's apricot kolacky. I haven't had one of those for years."

They parted ways as Charlotte headed toward the band to check with Clive to make sure the band was ready to go.

"We're all set," he told her. "Do you have a request for the first song? We can play just about anything from the forties and fifties."

Charlotte thought about it for a moment and then remembered her mother's favorite tune from her USO days. "Do you know 'The G.I. Jive'?"

Clive grinned. "It's one of our favorites."

Charlotte nodded, feeling it would be the perfect choice. "Okay, we can start with that one as soon as I welcome everyone."

She took the microphone. "Good evening. I want to welcome everyone to our very own USO dance. I'd like to introduce two very special guests tonight. They are Anita Wilson and Lydia Middleton."

She looked over the crowd, pleased to see the two women seated together. "They're sitting at the table under the scoreboard. Wave, ladies, so everyone can see you. They both served in the USO during World War II and will be judging our jitterbug contest later this evening."

Both women waved to the crowd who reacted with loud applause.

Charlotte began speaking again. "I'm sure there are veterans from other wars here tonight, as well as the men and women who loved and supported them. I want to honor you all and thank you for serving our country." She'd hoped that George Kimball would be here as well, but he'd said he didn't feel up to a dance without his Helen, but would try to take part in the ceremony and reenactment on Monday.

Her words provoked another long round of applause. She waited until it faded and then wrapped up her speech. "There's plenty of food, so help yourselves. Let's all have fun and dance the night away. This first song is dedicated to my mother, Opal Coleman, who loved her years in the USO." She turned to the band. "Take it away, boys."

The pianist started playing, and the rest of the band joined in, filling the gym with music. As Charlotte left the stage, Clive started swinging one arm back and forth and singing. "This is the G.I. Jive . . ."

EMILY WAITED FOR THE RIGHT TIME to make her escape. She checked the food table, making certain to remove any empty dishes and clean up food that had spilled over onto the table. Then she refilled the water and iced-tea coolers and restocked the paper plates, napkins, and cups.

Taking a quick look around the gym, she spotted her grandparents seated at a table with Frank and Hannah Carter. Good. They were so busy talking Grandma wouldn't notice her slipping out.

She was just about to leave through the back door of the kitchen when Great-Aunt Rosemary approached her. "You look like you could use a break."

Emily breathed a sigh of relief. "You have perfect timing."

"You go ahead," Rosemary told her. "I'll watch the food table until you get back."

"You're sure you don't mind?"

"Mind?" Rosemary placed a hand on her chest. "I'm still trying to catch my breath. I never expected anyone to ask me to dance tonight, and here I've been out on that dance floor for three songs in a row." She smiled at Emily. "Believe me, honey, I could use a break."

"Okay," Emily said, heading toward the door. "I'll try to be back soon."

"Take your time," Rosemary told her. "I'm having too much fun to leave anytime soon."

Emily removed her apron and set it on the kitchen counter and then walked through the back door. The sun had already set, and the only light was from the street lamp on the corner.

"Emily," a voice called from the shadows. "Over here."

She rounded the corner of the school and almost bumped into Troy. "Why are you hiding?"

"I didn't want anyone to see me. I still can't believe I'm doing this."

"You promised me, remember? Do you have everything you need?"

"I think so." Troy picked up the blue duffel bag beside him. "Are you sure you still want to go through with this? It's not too late to back out."

"I'm sure," Emily said without hesitation. She wasn't about to chicken out now. "Let's go."

"HOW DO YOU THINK IT'S GOING?" Charlotte asked Hannah.

"Perfect!" Hannah exclaimed. "I feel like I've been transported back in time. The band is great. I've been tapping my toes all evening."

"You and Frank should dance."

She laughed. "There's not a chance of that happening, I'm afraid. I think the last time we danced together was at our wedding."

Bob and Frank were too engrossed in their conversation about grain prices to pay much attention. It just proved to Charlotte that Bob might not be working on the farm anymore but it was still in his blood.

"How about you and Bob?" Hannah said. "Are you entering the jitterbug contest together?"

"Oh, heavens no," Charlotte said. "You know Bob better than that. Our husbands are a lot alike, Hannah. They hung up their dancing shoes a long time ago."

"Are Bill and Anna coming tonight?"

"No, I'm afraid not." Charlotte took a sip of her tea. "Will has a case of the sniffles again, so they decided to stay home. I'm hoping the baby's well enough for the whole family to come to Bedford on Monday. Jennifer and Madison are so excited about the festivities."

"So Bill might miss participating in the war reenactment?"

"No, he told me he's coming either way. I don't think he'd miss it for the world." She wished Pete felt the same way, but Charlotte had accepted the fact that he wouldn't be joining the rest of the Stevenson and Slater men in the reenactment.

She looked around the gym, wondering if Pete and Dana had arrived yet. Sam had taken Christopher home a little while ago. She was surprised they'd stayed at the dance as long as they had, but she knew the abundance of food had been a big draw for both boys.

She suddenly spotted Pete and Dana near the front

entrance where they were talking to Brad Weber and his date. Dana was the only one of the four dressed in forties-style clothing, but that didn't matter to Charlotte. She was just glad they'd come.

"I'm going to round up Anita and Lydia," Charlotte told Hannah. "It will be time for the jitterbug contest soon."

Hannah stood up with her. "While you do that, I think I'll take another trip to the food table. Did you try Andrea Vink's war bread?"

"Not yet. Is it good?"

"Good doesn't begin to describe it. That bread melts in your mouth. I've just got to get that recipe from her. War rations or not, her bread is delicious."

Charlotte laughed. "I think there are going to be a lot of recipe exchanges around Bedford. Maybe we should print a cookbook."

Hannah's eyes widened. "Hey, that's not a bad idea. A cookbook of vintage recipes. We could sell it for a fund-raiser at church."

"Oh, no," Charlotte said, laughing as she backed away. "I've taken on enough projects for a while. After this dance is over, I need a good, long rest."

"I hear you. Maybe we should just put the idea on the back burner for now."

Charlotte thought she spotted Anita through the crowd. "I've gotta run. See you in a bit."

"I'll save a seat for you," Hannah called after her.

Charlotte hurried over to Anita. "Are you ready to judge the dance?"

"I sure am," Anita told her, "even if it is a little bit past my bedtime. Lydia and I have been talking about the old

USO days. This dance really brings back some wonderful memories."

"I'm so glad to hear it," Charlotte said, looking for Lydia. "Where is she, by the way?"

"Over at the food table talking to Rosemary. Do you want me to fetch her?"

"I can do it," Charlotte replied. "I'll need you both sitting by the dance floor so you can have a good view of all the dancers in the contest."

Anita chuckled. "Let's get started then."

"Do you need any help?"

"I'll be fine," Anita assured her.

Charlotte walked over to the food table, eager to escort Lydia to the dance floor so they could start the contest.

"There she is," Rosemary proclaimed as Charlotte walked up, "the woman who made this all possible. Charlotte, I have to thank you for talking me into coming tonight. I can't remember when I've had so much fun."

"You're welcome. I'm glad you're having a good time." Charlotte noticed Rosemary was the only person manning the food table. "Where's Emily?"

"I told her to take a break." Rosemary glanced at her watch. "She's been gone quite a while so I'm sure she'll be back soon."

"If she's not, I'll go look for her after the jitterbug contest. Right now, I'd better get to the microphone."

Charlotte helped Lydia and Anita to their seats just as the band was finishing up a song. She signaled to the band leader, and he handed her the microphone. "Ladies and gentleman, it's time for our jitterbug contest."

A joyous shout went up from the crowd. Several couples

came onto the floor, and Charlotte waited a few moments so that everyone who wanted to participate could make it to the dance floor on time.

"The contest will last until the song is over, and then we'll announce the winners." She turned to Anita and Lydia. "Are you ready, judges?"

Anita gave her a thumbs-up. "We're ready."

Charlotte turned back to the crowd. "Let's jitterbug!"

The band broke into a rousing rendition of "Boogie Woogie Bugle Boy," and all the couples began to dance. That's when Charlotte saw Emily, although she barely recognized her. She was right in the middle of the dance floor with Troy, and they were both dancing the jitterbug like they were born to it.

Troy wore a full army uniform, looking every bit the soldier from the cap on his head to the boots on his feet. Emily looked adorable in her vintage green dress with her hair done up exactly like her grandmother Opal wore hers during her USO days.

Charlotte put a hand up to her chest, her heart touched as she watched them dance their hearts out. They both had big smiles on their faces, and Charlotte could imagine her mother and father looking just the same eighty years ago.

She wondered why Emily hadn't told her that she and Troy were entering the contest. From the way they were moving, this wasn't the first time they'd danced the jitterbug together.

When the song ended, Lydia and Anita conferred for a few minutes and then handed their results to Charlotte.

"Congratulations," Charlotte said into the microphone. "You all did a marvelous job, but three couples stood out from the crowd." She looked down at the paper. "In third place, Marcus and Stacie Lindstrom!" She waited a moment while the crowd applauded as the Lindstroms received their trophy.

"In second place," Charlotte continued, so excited that the paper shook in her hands, "Emily Slater and Troy Vanderveen!"

Charlotte smiled when she saw Emily jumping up and down as she and Troy picked up their trophy.

"And in first place, David and Sarah Carr!"

Charlotte handed the microphone back to the band leader and then helped Anita and Lydia off the stage before going in search of her granddaughter.

Emily found her first. "Did you see us, Grandma? We won second place!"

"I sure *did* see you." She looked between Troy and Emily. "I couldn't believe my eyes."

"I wanted to surprise you," Emily said. "I figured that was the least I could do after . . . everything."

Charlotte looked at Troy. "And you went along with it?"

Troy shrugged. "I really didn't have a choice."

Emily laughed. "Remember when I told you Troy had offered to take me on a special date of my choosing? This is what I picked."

Now Charlotte was the one laughing. "Poor Troy. Look what you got yourself into."

"I know," he said, looking a little embarrassed. "I just hope none of my friends find out."

"But where did you two learn to dance like that?" Charlotte asked.

Emily smiled. "We found some online video lessons for the jitterbug on the Internet and memorized the steps, and then we practiced every chance we got. Including the day of Sam's graduation party."

"You mean . . ." Charlotte's voice trailed off as the pieces finally fit together.

"That's what we were doing in my bedroom when you found us," Emily said, her eyes dancing with mischief. "We'd already planned to enter the jitterbug contest, and I wanted to surprise you."

"Well, you certainly did just that."

"So you liked it?"

Charlotte reached out to give her a hug. "I loved it!"

Soon after the contest was over the band leader announced that the dance was coming to an end. "For our last song of the evening," the band leader said, "we invite you to come along as we take you on a sentimental journey."

The band began to play the song "Sentimental Journey," and Charlotte began to hum along to the familiar strains. The USO dance had been a huge success, thanks to the help of all her wonderful volunteers.

Someone tapped her on the shoulder. She turned around to see Bob standing behind her.

He held out his hand. "May I have this dance?"

"You want to dance? With me?"

"That's why I asked, isn't it?" He led her onto the dance floor and then pulled her into his arms as they swayed to the music together.

"But you don't like to dance," Charlotte said, still stunned that he'd asked her.

"Frank and I heard you girls talking about us hanging up our dancing shoes, so we thought we'd prove you wrong."

She looked over to see Hannah dancing with her husband. She looked just as shocked to be on the dance floor as Charlotte was. But the shock soon faded as they danced with their husbands, and Charlotte found herself enjoying every moment of their own sentimental journey.

Chapter Twenty-Seven

On Sunday, Charlotte was tired, but it was a good tired. They'd all gone to church together as a family, and then she'd served leftovers for dinner. Not the best meal for a Sunday dinner but they'd all filled up on food last night so no one complained too much.

"What are we doing the rest of the day?" Emily asked.

"Relaxing," Charlotte said. "I might even take a nap this afternoon."

"That sounds good to me too," Bob said. "I want to be well rested before the big day tomorrow."

"What time do we need to be there for the reenactment?" Sam asked him.

"It starts at ten o'clock sharp. I'm going in earlier to get everything set up."

Sam reached for another dinner roll. "Do you want me to go in with you?"

"Sure," Bob replied. "I could use the help."

Charlotte took a sip of her coffee, wondering what time Bill would arrive tomorrow. "Do you think Bill will be coming here first or going straight to the reenactment site?"

Bob shrugged. "I don't know. I'll give him a call later on this afternoon and find out."

"Tell him to bring the girls even if Anna and Will can't come. I'll watch them until he's through with the reenactment."

"Will do," Bob said.

Charlotte leaned back in her chair, comfortably full from dinner. It was hard to believe the month was almost over. Sam had graduated, and Emily and Christopher were done now too.

Summer would probably fly by just as fast, and then Sam would be going off to Central Community College in Grand Island in the fall. He'd take his general education classes first and wait to decide what field he wanted to go into. She hoped his being around the other college students would give him some ideas.

"Do we have any pie left?" Bob asked, referring to the practice cherry-berry pie Charlotte had made before the USO dance.

"There are two pieces left," Charlotte said. "Who wants them?"

"Me," Bob and Sam said at the same time.

Charlotte looked at her husband. "Are you sure about that? You've been doing so well on your diet—it would be a shame to stop now."

Bob scowled. "I'll just have half a piece, if that will make you happy."

"It will," she replied, rising from her chair to serve up the pie. "Anybody want the other half of Grandpa's piece? Emily? Christopher?"

"You can have it, Christopher," Emily told her brother. "I ate too much last night. That's the down side to manning the food table. You can't get away from temptation."

Emily had set her jitterbug trophy on the television in the family room. Troy had told her to keep it since the contest had been her idea in the first place.

"How about it, Christopher?" Charlotte said as she dished up half a slice of pie for Bob and then added a small scoop of ice cream to it. "Do you want some pie?"

"Maybe in a little while," Christopher said. He reached into his back pocket and pulled out a piece of paper. "Can I read you my story first?"

"Sure," Charlotte told him, carrying the dessert plates over to Sam and Bob. "Is this the newspaper story you wrote about George Kimball?"

"Yeah," Christopher replied, smoothing the crinkled paper on the table. "I'm supposed to read it at the war reenactment, and I want to make sure it sounds all right."

"Let me sit down before you start," Charlotte said, refilling Bob's coffee cup and then setting the pot back on the counter. She took her chair again. "Okay, I'm ready."

Christopher picked up the paper, cleared his throat twice, and began reading:

"Mr. George Kimball served in the army in World War II. He was twenty years old when he went to boot camp. He had only been married three days to his wife, Helen."

"You're talking too fast," Emily interjected. "Slow it down a little."

"Okay," Christopher said, finding his place in the story once more. "Helen planted a victory rosebush and promised it would be in bloom when he came home again. The roses are yellow, and a relative of that rosebush still blooms today."

Sam looked up from his pie. "A relative?"

Christopher frowned. "I don't know how else to say it. George told me they kept cutting off pieces of the bush and turning them into new bushes."

"It sounds like they propagated it," Charlotte said. "But I like your word, Christopher. Why don't you change it to, 'a propagated relative of that rosebush still lives today.'"

"Okay," Christopher said, taking a stubby pencil out of his shirt pocket and making the change. "I think that does sound better."

"George fought in France and said D-Day was really bad and a lot of men died. The thing I remember most from my interview with George is that wars are horrible and should only be fought when absolutely necessary. But he said some good things happened to him during the war too. He met lots of new friends from all over the country, and he got to see some neat things in Europe."

Christopher leaned down to make another correction with his pencil and then continued reading. "When I interviewed George I found out he had a lot in common with my great-grandpa, Les Stevenson, who also fought in World War II. They were both from Bedford. They were both married. They both believed that sometimes fighting was necessary even if it took you far away from home."

Charlotte found herself mesmerized by his story, finding so much truth in a child's simple words. The rest of the family had grown silent too, no longer critiquing his word choices or speaking skills.

"Both George and my Great-Grandpa Les believed they were fighting to make sure we all kept our freedoms and to protect people who couldn't protect themselves. Most of all, they were fighting to keep their families safe at home. That's what was most important to both of them. They loved their families more than anything and couldn't wait to get home again. I think everybody should remember that these soldiers fought for all of us and we should always cherish the things they were fighting for."

When Christopher was finished reading, nobody said a word. Charlotte glanced at Bob, who looked like he might have a tear in his eye, but she couldn't be sure.

"Well," Christopher asked, looking around the table, "is it all right?"

"I think it's perfect," Charlotte told him. "You did a nice job."

"Whew," Christopher said. "That's good, because I already turned it in to the school newspaper."

"You did a great job," Emily told her brother as she got up from the table. "I'm going to saddle up Princess and ride her this afternoon since we don't have any other plans. Anyone want to join me?"

"I will," Christopher said, jumping up from the table.

"How about it, Sam?" Emily asked. "Feel like doing a little horseback riding?"

"Sure." Sam carried his empty plate to the sink, and the other two followed him out the door.

Charlotte waited until they were gone and then turned to Bob. "What did you think of Christopher's story?"

"Out of the mouths of babes," Bob said with a sigh.

"Your dad truly loved his family."

Bob nodded. "That was always important to him, keeping the family together."

Charlotte let out a breath.

"I think I'll give Pete a call," Bob said, rising up from the table. "See if we can settle this thing once and for all."

Thank you, God, Charlotte prayed to herself, *for helping him see the light.*

"I'm afraid you're going to have to wait," Charlotte told him. "Pete and Dana drove to North Platte today to place flowers on her grandparents' graves. Dana told me they won't be back until late tonight."

Bob got up from the table. "Then I think I'll take an antacid and nap in my recliner for about an hour or so."

"An antacid?" Charlotte reached over to feel his forehead. "Don't you feel well?"

"I'm fine," Bob assured her. "I'm just preparing myself for the big dish of crow I'm going to be eating soon."

MEMORIAL DAY ARRIVED bright and clear on Heather Creek Farm. To Charlotte's regret, Bob had to leave to set up for the war reenactment before Pete came out to do chores. She didn't want another day to go by without the two of them reconciling.

Bob had called Bill last night and learned that Anna didn't think Will was well enough to spend the day in Bedford. Bill had promised to bring the girls with him and made arrangements to meet Charlotte in front of Mel's Place.

Sam and Emily were already in town. Sam had gone in with Bob, and Troy had picked Emily up early so they could help out at the church's bake sale at the park.

"Hey, Grandma," Christopher said as he walked into the

house. "I've got Magic in the livestock trailer, so we're ready whenever you are."

Charlotte was driving Christopher and his lamb into Bedford for the 4-H petting zoo. "Did you put his patriotic blanket on him?"

"Not yet," Christopher said. "I didn't want it to get dirty. I'm going to wait to put it on right before we get to the park."

"Where is it?"

"Emily took it with her when Troy picked her up this morning." Christopher walked over to the cookie jar and reached in for a cookie. "She wanted to sew some stars on it or something. She promised to give it to me at the park."

"All right," Charlotte said, walking over to the counter to turn off the coffeepot, "we'd better get going. The petting zoo is scheduled to start in an hour."

Christopher grabbed two more cookies before following her out the door. Charlotte drove Bob's pickup, pulling the trailer behind it; she parked a block from the park so her vehicle wouldn't be in the way.

"Put Magic's halter on him before you let him out of the trailer," Charlotte warned. "We don't want to be chasing him all over town."

"I know, Grandma," Christopher told her, scooting out the other side.

She stood by the back of the trailer and watched while Christopher put the halter on his lamb. She had to give him credit; he'd really tamed Magic. The lamb would probably follow him anywhere now, even without the halter. Not that she wanted to test that theory anytime soon.

"Okay," Christopher said from inside the livestock trailer. "I think we're ready."

Charlotte opened the trailer's gate, and Christopher led Magic out. The lamb looked around but didn't try to make a run for it. Charlotte took that as a good sign.

"I'll walk with you to the park," Charlotte told him. "Then you and Magic are on your own."

"Grandma," Christopher complained, "I'm not a little kid anymore. You don't have to walk me there. That would be so embarrassing."

She bit back a smile at his reaction, even as she realized he was right. Christopher was growing up. "Are you sure?"

"Positive," he replied.

"Okay. I'll see you in a little while." Charlotte reached down to pluck a piece of straw off Magic's ear. "We have to go straight to the war reenactment after we're done here, so don't dawdle."

"I won't," Christopher promised.

They parted ways, and Charlotte headed toward Mel's Place. She could hear the Bedford High marching band playing in the park and looked forward to taking the girls there. Rosemary had arranged some games for the children to play, and she knew Jennifer and Madison would have a lot of fun.

When she reached Mel's she was happy to see Bill and the girls were already there.

"Hello, sweeties," she said, embracing the girls. "Have you been waiting for me long?"

"No," Madison said. "Daddy took us inside the store to get some lollipops." She opened her mouth and stuck out her blue tongue. "See?"

"I'd guess you got a blue lollipop," Charlotte said, smiling as she turned to Jennifer. "And what color did you get?"

Jennifer stuck out her tongue.

"Orange." Charlotte looked at Bill. "And how about you?"

He laughed. "I think the last time I stuck my tongue out at you I got grounded for three days."

"Come on," she prodded. "Show me." Then she laughed when he flashed his green tongue at her. "Well, I'm glad to see you're all starting off the day with some nutritious lollipops."

"The girls each ate a good breakfast," Bill said, "so I figured a little candy wouldn't hurt them."

"Are you girls ready to go to the park and have fun?" Charlotte asked them.

"Yes!" they answered in unison, both jumping up and down.

"Thanks for watching them, Mom," Bob said. "I appreciate it."

"It's my pleasure," she replied; then she looked at her watch.

"You'd better get going so you can start getting situated for the reenactment. If I know your dad, he'll think you're already late."

"You're right about that." Bill bent down to give his girls a hug. "You two be good for Grandma. I'll see you in a little while."

"Bye, Daddy," the girls chorused as he walked away.

A loud drumbeat sounded in the distance, and Jennifer's eyes got very wide. "What's that?"

"It's the bass drum in the marching band. They're playing in the park. Shall we go see them?"

"Can we pet the animals there too?" Jennifer asked her.

"We sure can. Christopher is there with Magic. There are other animals there too, like rabbits and goats and baby calves."

"I want to pet a baby calf," Madison said.

They made their way to the park, where lots of people had already gathered. The high school dance team was putting on a performance near the bandstand while a clown juggled tennis balls near the bake-sale table.

Charlotte turned the girls toward the petting zoo. "There's Christopher and Magic."

The girls waved wildly when they saw Christopher. He stood with the other 4-H members in the cordoned-off petting zoo. When he saw Charlotte and the girls, he waved to them, a huge smile on his face.

Charlotte was relieved to see that Magic was perfectly behaved and looked quite handsome in his patriotic blanket.

"Are you having fun?" she asked him as the girls petted the animals around them.

"It's pretty cool," Christopher said. "Lots of people like Magic."

"I'm sure they do." Charlotte watched the girls move among the animals, wishing she'd remembered to bring her camera. After the petting zoo, they moved on to some of the children's games and spent the next hour absorbed in all the activities.

At the designated time, Charlotte took the girls to meet Christopher at the truck. They watched while he put Magic in the livestock trailer and then took off the lamb's halter before serving him a nice big wedge of alfalfa. "There,"

Christopher said. "That should keep him happy for a while."

"We'd better get to Paul Hubbard's place so your grandpa doesn't start wondering where you are."

"I need to change into my uniform first," Christopher told her.

"Grandpa has it with him. He said you can change in one of the tents."

"Okay," Christopher said, climbing into the truck.

Charlotte belted the girls in and then took off for the reenactment site. It took only a few minutes to get there, but she hardly recognized Paul Hubbard's land when she saw it.

"Look at that!" Christopher exclaimed.

Bob and his volunteers had transformed the area into an army camp, complete with tents and campfires and foxholes. It looked like something out of a war movie, especially with all the men walking around in their uniforms.

Charlotte and the kids got out of the truck and started walking toward the camp. She knew that once the reenactment officially started only the participants would be allowed in the camp. Everyone else would watch them from the bleachers set up near the road.

Bob, Bill, and Sam met them at the perimeter of the camp.

"Hey, there," Bill greeted his girls. "Did you have fun?"

"We sure did," Madison said. "I petted a baby calf, and it licked my hand."

Bob turned to Christopher. "You can go change in our tent. Sam will show you where it is."

"I want to see a tent too," Jennifer said. "Please, Daddy?"

"Okay, girls," Bill said, grabbing their hands. "But only for a few minutes." They followed Sam and Christopher to the center of the encampment area.

Charlotte looked around her in amazement. "Oh, Bob, this more authentic than I ever imagined."

"It's really something, isn't it?"

She looked over toward the truck to make sure Magic wasn't trying to find an escape route, only to see something that made her grab Bob's arm.

"It's Pete!" she said. "He's coming this way. And look what he's wearing!"

Bob followed her gaze and then cleared his throat. "Could it be Dad's old uniform?"

She watched their son march toward them wearing his grandfather's army uniform. It fit him perfectly.

Bob kept his eyes on his son until Pete was standing right in front of him.

"Is it too late to join the Stevenson unit?" Pete asked him.

Charlotte held her breath, praying that Bob would say the right thing. She knew how much it had taken for Pete to come here today.

"It's never too late for family," Bob told him. "I'm glad you're here, son. And I'm proud that you're wearing my dad's uniform."

Pete held out his arms. "It's like it was made for me."

"Maybe it was," Bob said thoughtfully.

Charlotte had been wondering the same thing. Was God's hand at work here?

"You know, Dad," Pete said, "I'm going to fall behind on

the farm if I spend all day out here with you. I'll need you to help me catch up."

Bob clapped him on the shoulder. "I thought you'd never ask. I was going stir-crazy sitting in the house all day, although it was probably no more than I deserved for making a boneheaded move like mixing corn herbicide with soybean herbicide."

"It was my fault," Pete said. "I should have marked the container more clearly or used another container instead. That was an accident waiting to happen."

"Why don't we each take 50 percent of the blame," Bob suggested, "and just call it even?"

"Deal," Pete said, shaking his hand.

Charlotte was able to hold back her tears until Bob and Pete walked away. God had answered her prayers in the most wonderful way possible.

As she watched the war reenactment, Charlotte could see a special connection forming between her husband, sons, and grandsons. Even though Les wasn't here with them today, his enduring values—love of God, country, and family—had been passed down to the next generations.

About the Author

Kristin Eckhardt is the author of more than fifty books, including twenty-four novels for Guideposts. She has won two national awards for her writing and her first book was made into a television movie. When she isn't writing, Kristin enjoys traveling with her husband and spending time with their grandchildren.

A Note from the Editors

We hope you enjoyed this volume in the Home to Heather Creek series, published by Guideposts. For over seventy-five years, Guideposts, a nonprofit organization, has been driven by a vision of a world filled with hope. We aspire to be the voice of a trusted friend, a friend who makes you feel more hopeful and connected.

By making a purchase from Guideposts, you join our community in touching millions of lives, inspiring them to believe that all things are possible through faith, hope, and prayer. Your continued support allows us to provide uplifting resources to those in need.

Whether through our online communities, websites, apps, or publications, we strive to inspire our audiences, bring them together, and comfort, uplift, entertain, and guide them.

To learn more, please go to guideposts.org.

Find inspiration, find faith, find Guideposts.

Shop our best sellers and favorites at
guideposts.org/shop

Or scan the QR code to go directly to our Shop